THE
PARIS
MAPGUIDE
Michael Middleditch

W9-AUL-066

CONTENTS

The Maps in this Guide are based on the Plan de Paris édités par la Mairie de Paris, Direction de la Construction et du Logement with an original Ground Survey carried out by Michael Graham Publications.

PENGUIN BOOKS

2

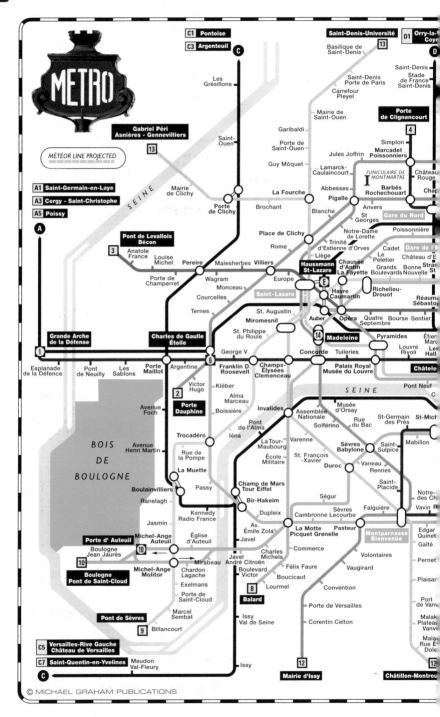

METRO

MÉTÉOR LINE PROJECTED

C1 Pontoise
C3 Argenteuil
C

Saint-Denis-Université
Basilique de Saint-Denis
13
D1 Orry-la-Coye
D

Les Grésillons

Saint-Denis Porte de Paris
Carrefour Pleyel

Saint-Denis Stade de France Saint-Denis

Gabriel Péri
Asnières - Gennevilliers

Saint-Ouen

13

Mairie de Saint-Ouen

Garibaldi

Porte de Saint-Ouen

Jules Joffrin

Porte de Clignancourt

4

Simplon
Marcadet Poissonniers

Guy Môquet

Lamarck-Caulaincourt

FUNICULAIRE DE MONTMARTRE

Château Rouge

A1 Saint-Germain-en-Laye
A3 Cergy - Saint-Christophe
A5 Poissy

A

SEINE

Mairie de Clichy

Porte de Clichy

La Fourche

Brochant

Abbesses

Pigalle

Blanche

Barbès Rochechouart

Anvers
St Georges

Chap

Gare du Nord

Place de Clichy

Notre-Dame de Lorette

Poissonnière

Gare de l'E

Pont de Levallois Bécon

3

Anatole France
Louise Michel

Pereire

Maleisherbes Villiers

Rome

Trinité d'Estienne d'Orves
Liège

Haussmann St-Lazare

Chausée d'Antin La Fayette

Cadet
Le Peletier
Grands Boulevards

Château d'E
Bonne Stras
Nouvelle St

Porte de Champerret

Wagram

Monceau

Europe

Saint-Lazare

E

Havre Caumartin

Richelieu-Drouot

Réaum
Sébasto

Courcelles

Ternes

Miromesnil

St. Augustin

Auber

Opéra

Quatre Septembre

Bourse

Sentier

Grande Arche de la Défense

Charles de Gaulle Étoile

St. Philippe du Roule

14

Madeleine

Pyramides

Étien
Marc
Les
Hall

1

Esplanade de la Défence

Pont de Neuilly

Les Sablons

Porte Maillot

Argentine

6

George V

Franklin D. Roosevelt

Champs-Élysées Clemenceau

Concorde

Tuileries

Palais Royal Musée du Louvre

Louvre
Rivoli

Châtele

Victor Hugo

Kléber

SEINE

Pont Neuf

C

2

Porte Dauphine

Alma Marceau

Boissière

Invalides

Assemblée Nationale
Solférino

Musée d'Orsay
Rue du Bac

St-Germain des Prés

St-Mich

Avenue Foch

Trocadéro

Iéna

Pont de l'Alma

La Tour-Maubourg

Varenne

Sèvres Babylone

Saint-Sulpice

Mabillon

BOIS DE BOULOGNE

Avenue Henri Martin

Rue de la Pompe

École Militaire

St. François -Xavier

Duroc

Vaneau

Rennes

La Muette

Passy

Champ de Mars Tour Eiffel

Ségur

Saint-Placide

Notre-des Ch

Boulainvilliers

Ranelagh

Bir-Hakeim

Dupleix

Cambronne Lecourbe

Sèvres

Falguière

Vavin R

Jasmin

Kennedy Radio France

Av. Émile Zola

La Motte Picquet Grenelle

Pasteur

Montparnasse Bienvenüe

Edgar Quinet

Porte d' Auteuil

Michel-Ange Auteuil

Église d'Auteuil

Javel

Commerce

Volontaires

Gaîté

Pernet

Boulogne Jean Jaurès

10

Charles Michels

Javel André Citroën

Félix Faure

Vaugirard

Boulogne Pont de Saint-Cloud

10

Michel-Ange Molitor

Chardon Lagache

Mirabeau

Boulevard Victor

Boucicaut

Convention

Plaisar

Exelmans

8

Balard

Lourmel

Porte de Versailles

Port de Van

Pont de Sèvres

Porte de Saint-Cloud

Marcel Sembat

Issy Val de Seine

Corentin Celton

Malak Platea Vanve

9

Billancourt

Mala Rue E Dole

C5 Versailles-Rive Gauche Château de Versailles

C7 Saint-Quentin-en-Yvelines

Meudon Val-Fleury

C

Issy

12

Mairie d'Issy

Châtillon-Montrou

13

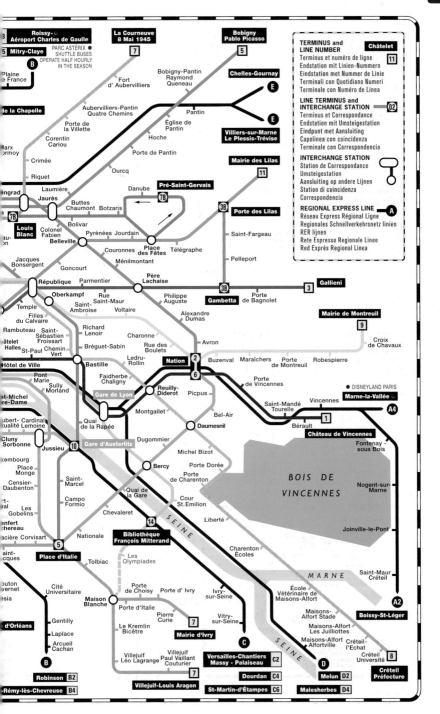

3

Roissy-Aéroport Charles de Gaulle
3
Mitry-Claye
5
B
PARC ASTÉRIX ● SHUTTLE BUSES OPERATE HALF HOURLY IN THE SEASON

Plaine France

de la Chapelle

Marx Dormoy

Crimée

Riquet

ingrad

Jaurès
Laumière

7B

Louis Blanc

Colonel Fabien

Jacques Bonsergent

République

Temple

Filles du Calvaire

Rambuteau
Saint-Sébastien Froissart

âtelet Halles
St-Paul

Hôtel de Ville

Pont Marie

t-Michel re-Dame

ubert- Cardinal tualité Lemoine

Cluny Sorbonne

cembourg

Place Monge

Censier-Daubenton

t- val

Les Gobelins

enfert chereau

acière Corvisart

aint- cques

outon vernet

esia

d'Orléans

La Courneuve 8 Mai 1945
7

Fort d'Aubervilliers

Aubervilliers-Pantin Quatre Chemins

Porte de la Villette

Corentin Cariou

Porte de Pantin

Ourcq

Danube

Buttes Chaumont Botzaris

Bolivar

Pyrénées Jourdain

Belleville

Goncourt

Parmentier

Oberkampf

Saint-Ambroise

Rue Saint-Maur

Voltaire

Richard Lenoir

Chemin Vert

Bréguet-Sabin

Bastille

Faidherbe Chaligny

Sully Morland

Quai de la Rapée

Gare de Lyon

Gare d'Austerlitz

Jussieu
10

Saint-Marcel

Campo Formio

Chevaleret

Nationale

Bibliothèque François Mitterrand
14

Place d'Italie
5

Tolbiac

Cité Universitaire

Maison Blanche

Porte d'Italie

Le Kremlin Bicêtre

Gentilly

Laplace

Arcueil Cachan

B

Robinson **B2**

-Rémy-lès-Chevreuse **B4**

Bobigny-Pantin Raymond Queneau

Pantin

Église de Pantin

Hoche

Bobigny Pablo Picasso
5

Chelles-Gournay
E

Villiers-sur-Marne Le Plessis-Trévise
E

Pré-Saint-Gervais
7B

Couronnes

Ménilmontant

Place des Fêtes

Télégraphe

Père Lachaise

Philippe Auguste

Gambetta

Charonne

Rue des Boulets

Ledru-Rollin

Reuilly-Diderot

Montgallet

Picpus

Dugommier

Bercy

Michel Bizot

Porte Dorée

Porte de Charenton

Quai de la Gare

Cour St.Emilion

Les Olympiades

Porte de Choisy

Pierre Curie

Porte d'Ivry

Mairie des Lilas
11

Porte des Lilas
3B

Saint-Fargeau

Pelleport

Porte de Bagnolet

Alexandre Dumas

Nation
2
6

Avron

Buzenval

Maraîchers

Porte de Montreuil

Robespierre

Porte de Vincennes

Saint-Mandé Tourelle

Vincennes

Bel-Air

Daumesnil

Bérault

Château de Vincennes

Liberté

Charenton Écoles

Ivry-sur-Seine

Vitry-sur-Seine

Mairie d'Ivry

Versailles-Chantiers Massy - Palaiseau **C2**

Dourdan **C4**

Villejuif Léo Lagrange

Villejuif Paul Vaillant Couturier

Villejuif-Louis Aragon
7

St-Martin-d'Étampes **C6**

Gallieni
3

Mairie de Montreuil
9

Croix de Chavaux

Marne-la-Vallée
A4
● DISNEYLAND PARIS

1

Fontenay sous Bois

Nogent-sur-Marne

Joinville-le-Pont

Saint-Maur Créteil

École Vétérinaire de Maisons-Alfort

Maisons-Alfort Stade

Maisons-Alfort Les Juilliottes

Maisons-Alfort Alfortville

C

Melun **D2**

Malesherbes **D4**

Boissy-St-Léger
A2

Créteil-l'Echat

Créteil Université
8

Créteil Préfecture

D

SEINE

MARNE

BOIS DE VINCENNES

PROLOGUE

Everybody remembers their first time in a foreign country. I was lucky my first venture abroad was to Paris. I was seventeen years old and the year was 1953. My companion was my grandmother, who had paid a substantial part of the holiday cost. We went from Victoria Station via Newhaven-Dieppe. I will never forget my first impressions, particularly the arrival at St. Lazare station on that hot August evening. It was the strange aroma of French perfume and Gauloises cigarettes that tantalised my senses. I hardly slept that first night, and when dawn came I got up and walked to the place de Clichy alone. Everywhere there was activity; water cleaning the streets, and many people in the cafés drinking coffee. As I wandered back to our hotel my thoughts were eagerly anticipating the experiences before me. Most days I arranged to meet my grandmother in the large department store 'Au Printemps' for dinner. We had a trip to to Versailles together. Mostly we went separate ways: she went to the 'Moulin Rouge', while I sat in stalls of the magnificent Garnier Opera House watching Verdi's 'Othello' on the huge stage. We went to the top of the Eiffel Tower and I swam in the Seine at the Piscine Deligny. I was introduced to Kronenbourg beer by two young men who took me to a chansonnier in Pigalle. Later that evening they deposited a happy boy back in the hotel on the rue de Moscou. I guess they did not want to be responsible for the consequences. I think my grandmother had put them up to taking me out - probably to increase my worldly knowledge! I went to the Vieux-Colombier, the famous jazz cellar in St. Germain where Sidney Bechet played, and I remember walking back by the Seine with the haunting image of Leslie Caron in 'An American in Paris' in my mind - nearly 40 years later, during the making of this Mapguide, I stood next to her in a shop in the rue de Rennes. When my grandmother went to the 'Folies Bergère', I went to see 'For whom the Bell Tolls' at the Paramount cinema. By this time I was falling in love with shop assistants and usherettes, always hoping they would talk to me in the lovely broken English that so many French entertainers seemed to use. Of course, this was my youth, and I am glad to say that Paris was part of it. Everytime I go to Paris, and I have been many times, I still get a feeling of excitement. Unlike many large cities, Paris has still retained its character. I cannot admit to enjoying the subterranean shopping centre of Les Halles or the intestinal Pompidou Centre, but these are only minor scars, for the heart remains.

A CITY IS BORN

300 years before the Romans came to Gaul, a small Celtic tribe of boatmen, fishermen and hunters called the Parisii lived on the island now known as the Île de la Cité. After Julius Cæsar's conquest in 52 BC, a camp was established, which later grew into a town that stretched across to the Left Bank and was called Lutetia. It was important both strategically and commercially as it was close to the junction of arterial rivers. The town was open, and the S-N axis ran along the present line of the rue St. Jacques, crossing the Pont Notre-Dame going towards the rue St. Martin. In the third century AD, the principal public buildings - a large forum, three thermal baths, and a theatre and arena had been built - which were supplemented by a water supply carried on an aqueduct from a source 15 kilometres to the south. The remains of the Cluny thermal baths and the arena can be seen today (Map Ref. Page 40, B4 and D6). The population at that time is estimated at between 6-9000 inhabitants. During the reign of the Emperor Julian the Apostate, the city became known as Parisea Civitus. By the end of the third century, Germanic invasions had forced the people back to the Île, where a citadel was built.

THE TWO HILLS

The Butte Montmartre (the Mount of the Martyrs) lies to the north and is today crowned by the Sacré Cœur. On this hill, St. Denis, the first Bishop of Paris, and his companions, Rusticus and Eleutherus, were martyred and buried. Later, a shrine was raised by Geneviève, who gives her name to the other hill (Montaigne Ste. Geneviève), on the south side of the city where the Panthéon now stands. The nearby church of St. Étienne du Mont (C6 40) is dedicated to Ste. Geneviève, Patron of Paris, and her tomb and shrine are there. Geneviève organised the defense of Paris against Attila the Hun, and later advised the people to surrender to Clovis, King of the Franks, who was a Christian and the first of the Merovingian dynasty. In AD 508, he beat and expelled the Romans, and made Paris his capital. The Franks or Freemen had been living on the east bank of the Rhine, and were Germans who had settled among Gauls and Romans; the French language came from the mixing of these three races.

THE FOUNTAINHEAD

After surviving onslaughts by Norsemen raiding up the river, Paris increased its importance under the early Capetian Kings (987-1328). Their palace was on the Île, and the towers of the Conciergerie are what remains of the building (B2 40).

King Philippe II (1189-1228), Philippe Auguste, built the famous city wall, beside which he built the moated château called Louvre, as a fortress to defend the river. Today, the unearthed base of the Grosse Tour can be seen in the depths of the Louvre museum. During Philippe's reign streets were paved, the University was founded, and the choir of Notre-Dame cathedral was completed. But above all these achievements, he is remembered most for being responsible for unifying the Franks.

By the end of the 14th century, Charles V extended the fortifications; he enclosed the faubourgs, or suburbs, by adding a new wall on the Right Bank. The Louvre was then made into a palace.

Paris was now the fountainhead of European learning as the schools of the Left Bank merged into the Sorbonne. In 1431, Henry VI of England was crowned King of France in Notre-Dame cathedral. The country had been occupied by the English for eleven years prior to the coronation. In 1437, however, France was recaptured by the French.

A CITY OF RENAISSANCE

The architecture of Paris: the infamous Bastille, Notre-Dame, as well as the Sainte Chapelle and many other churches were now established features on the skyline of the city. By 1546 the Louvre was considered too outmoded to be the palace; so it was decided to demolish and rebuild. All over Paris there were signs of of building, and Henry IV is identified with this resurgence: the place des Vosges (G2 41) dates from this period, as well as the Pont Neuf, where you can see the equestrian statue of Henri IV backed by the square du Vert Galant (A2 40).

The reign of Louis XIV (1643-1715),'Le Roi Soleil' (the Sun King), is synonymous with the spread of lavish industries. Everything associated with taste and intellect was concentrated in Paris during this period, but at the same time the seeds of Revolution were beginning to germinate.

REVOLUTION - REPUBLIC - NAPOLEON

France had helped the Americans in their War of Independence, and many noble ideas were adapted for French use when the time came in 1789. On the 14th of July, the Bastille, the great fortress prison which dominated Paris, was attacked by the mob, and at a later date levelled to the ground. When the National Convention sat in 1792, they abolished the monarchy and the Republic was born. The King and Queen were guillotined and within two years the revolutionary leaders, Robespierre and Danton, were to join them! The Royalists in 1795 were still not completely beaten: they tried to march against the Convention and were routed by Napoleon Bonaparte. The next year, he was put in command of the Army for the 'Italian Campaign'. The National Convention was replaced by the Directory, and Napoleon, because of his successful Italian and Egyptian campaigns, was able to take power. He became Emperor of France in 1804. Napoleon then proceeded to modernise Paris: the Madeleine and two triumphal arches - the Arc du Carrousel and the Arc de Triomphe - were built. At the same time, the arcaded rue de Rivoli and many other streets were laid out. After a brief comeback and then his final defeat at Waterloo, Napoleon was forced to abdicate and spent the rest of his life interned on the island of St. Helena, where he died in 1821. The civil code established by the Revolution and carried out by Napoleon had done away with feudalism, tolerated persons of all religions, modernised the tax and legal systems, and had an effect all over the world. After this period, great men of literature, art and music came to live in Paris, making it the cultural centre of the world.

BARON HAUSSMANN

The 2nd Republic was proclaimed in 1848, and Louis Napoleon III, the nephew of Bonaparte, was made Emperor four years later. Emperors build, and Louis had an excellent town planner in Baron Haussmann. The one unfortunate part of his architectural vigour is that so much of medieval Paris was to disappear when the Baron bisected Paris with the great avenues and boulevards. On the positive side, he cleared untidy dumps and waste ground and sculpted them into beautiful parks. Less romantic, but nevertheless important, was the vast underground network of sewers he was responsible for. With the advent of the railways, stations began to encircle the old city. The layout of the boulevards radiating from rond-points and the height of the buildings of Paris are credited as part of his concept. Haussmann was able to transform Paris, but because of the considerable expense involved, his opponents were able to force him to resign in 1869. Although Haussmann had gone, many of his projects were still being fulfilled in the early 1900s.

LA BELLE ÉPOQUE

During the late 19th century, France was at war with Prussia, and in 1870 Paris was besieged. Napoleon III was exiled to England where he lived in Chislehurst, in Kent! When the siege was lifted, Paris was occupied by Germans for three days. A National Government was set up at Versailles and at the same time the revolutionary Commune government was established in Paris. As a result civil war broke out and Paris was under siege again. Many thousands of people died on the barricades and in the reprisals that followed. When the fighting finished, the damage was assessed and in a comparatively short time restoration was achieved. The Grand Opera House, which was designed by Charles Garnier, and now bears his name, was started in 1861 and finished in 1875. On the boulevards, many famous cafes and restaurants were established. Three world fairs encouraged more building, and from one of these the Eiffel Tower emerged, to become a symbol of Paris. By 1914 the Sacré Cœur was finally completed and the finishing touches were put to the hill of Montmartre. From the mid 19th century until World War One, elegance and gaiety characterised Parisian life: the Can-Can, the risqué dance displayed at the Moulin Rouge, was unparalleled. Toulouse Lautrec immortalised the cabaret in his paintings and lithographs. Montmartre became the centre for the artistic colony, but by the 1920s, Montparnasse on the Left Bank had become the new focal point. Art studios and cafés, now places for modern pilgrims, blossomed. Art-nouveau began to flourish and was taken up in the design of the Metro entrances: an example is Abbesses station (H3 23). The elegant 16th arrondissement is the area where most of the architecture in this style is concentrated.

PARIS TODAY

Surviving two world wars and the German occupation between 1940 and 1944, the architecture of the city was not greatly damaged. Paris is still the centre of fashion and art of all descriptions, a sublime catalyst, the capital of Intellect and Love.

Arrondissements

The centre of Paris is divided into 20 districts or arrondissements. Each has its own administrative system, with a Prefect or Mayor, and a Council to manage its affairs, which are conducted in the Mairie or Town Hall. Usually, a police station is close by. The Prefect of the whole city resides in the Town Hall of Paris - the Hôtel de Ville (D2 40) in the 4th arrondissement. If you want to find out what is happening in the city, go to the Hôtel de Ville. For local information, go to the Mairie where you are situated.

LOCATION OF TOWN HALLS

1	Louvre	A6 32	11	Popincourt	C1 42
2	Bourse	A4 32	12	Reuilly*	D2 48
3	Temple	F5 33	13	Gobelins	E5 47
4	Hôtel de Ville	E2 41	14	Observatoire	E5 45
5	Panthéon	B6 40	15	Vaugirard*	A1 44
6	Luxembourg	G4 39	16	Passy	A5 28
7	Palais Bourbon	D2 38	17	Batignolles	D3 22
8	Élysée	C6 22	18	Montmartre*	B1 24
9	Opéra	A2 32	19	Buttes Chaumont	C4 26
10	Entrepôt	E2 33	20	Ménilmontant	H4 35

*an asterisk indicates the Town Hall is off the map area

THE LOUVRE

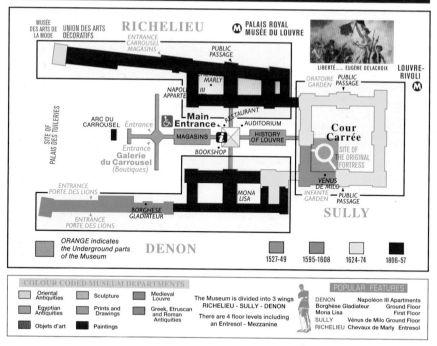

MUSÉE DES ARTS DE LA MODE — UNION DES ARTS DÉCORATIFS

RICHELIEU

ENTRANCE CARROUSEL MAGASINS

PUBLIC PASSAGE

Ⓜ PALAIS ROYAL MUSÉE DU LOUVRE

LIBERTÉ...... EUGÈNE DELACROIX

LOUVRE-RIVOLI Ⓜ

ORATOIRE GARDEN — PUBLIC PASSAGE

THÉÂTRE MARLY III

NAPOL APPARTE

ARC DU CARROUSEL — Entrance

SITE OF PALAIS DES TUILERIES

♿ **Main Entrance**

RESTAURANT

AUDITORIUM

MAGASINS

ℹ️

HISTORY OF LOUVRE

Cour Carrée

SITE OF THE ORIGINAL FORTRESS

Entrance
Galerie du Carrousel
(Boutiques)

BOOKSHOP

ENTRANCE PORTE DES LIONS

MONA LISA

VÉNUS DE MILO

INFANTE GARDEN — PUBLIC PASSAGE

SULLY

ENTRANCE PORTE DES LIONS

BORGHÈSE GLADIATEUR

DENON

ORANGE indicates the Underground parts of the Museum

1527-49   1595-1608   1624-74   1806-57

COLOUR CODED MUSEUM DEPARTMENTS

Oriental Antiquities	Sculpture	Medieval Louvre
Egyptian Antiquities	Prints and Drawings	Greek, Etruscan and Roman Antiquities
Objets d'art	Paintings	

The Museum is divided into 3 wings
RICHELIEU - SULLY - DENON

There are 4 floor levels including an Entresol - Mezzanine

POPULAR FEATURES

DENON — Napoléon III Apartments
Borghèse Gladiateur — Ground Floor
Mona Lisa — First Floor
SULLY — Vénus de Milo Ground Floor
RICHELIEU Chevaux de Marly — Entresol

See Map 31 Square H6

The original Louvre fortress was built in the reign of Philippe Auguste in the late 12th century. The foundations of this castle were unearthed during the more recent excavations underneath the Cour Carrée. They can be viewed on the mezzanine level after entering the Pyramid. On the way you pass a display depicting the history of the Louvre up to the modern day Pyramid. After Charles V (1364-80) had extended the city wall, the castle was used as a palace. By 1546 the old fortress was considered outmoded for this purpose, so the King, François I, ordered Pierre Lescot to build a new palace on the same site. Henri II continued the work, and Pierre Lescot's design was incorporated into a grander design in keeping with the classical spirit. The Tuileries Palace was commissioned by Catherine de Medici in 1564 and was connected to the Louvre by the 'Grande Galerie', now called Denon. In the 17th century, Louis XIII and 'le Roi Soleil' - Louis XIV built round the Cour Carrée a three storey elevation, with a colonnade on the east side. It is interesting that during the Revolution a Pyramid with the many names of people massacred by the monarchy was temporarily erected in the Tuileries gardens in front of the Tuileries Palace; adjoining which Napoleon and later Napoleon III had the north wing, (now known as Richelieu) built symmetrical to the 'Grande Galerie', thereby enclosing the space. The Communards, in their desperation, set fire to the Tuileries Palace causing irreparable damage, so it was decided to level it.

At the height of the Revolution in 1793, the 'Grande Galerie' was declared a museum; with Napoleon's conquests it began to fill up with treasures.

Over the years more display rooms have been made available. Today the Louvre has a main entrance - the Pyramid, and a labyrinth that extends over 700 metres, designed by the Chinese-American, Ieoh Ming Pei. Its archeological collection is one of the richest in the world, and the paintings include a great number of Italian 16th century masterpieces, and many from the early French School. Leonardo da Vinci, Michelangelo, Botticelli, Claude Lorrain, Rembrandt, Watteau, Louis David, and Eugène Delacroix, among many others, can be seen.

SULLY
GROUND FLOOR   Antiquities - Oriental Greek, Egyptian, Roman. 🚻 10-17a
FIRST FLOOR   Antiquities - Objets d'Art Greek, Etruscan, Egyptian, Roman. 🚻 22-38-43
SECOND FLOOR   French Painting XIV - XVII - XVIII - XIX Century 🚻 32-44-60
DENON
GROUND FLOOR   Antiquities - Greek, Etruscan Sculpture - Italian and Northern
FIRST FLOOR   Antiquities - Objets d'Art Paintings - French, Italian and Spanish 🚻 8
SECOND FLOOR   Temporary Exhibitions
RICHELIEU
GROUND FLOOR   Islamic Antiquities (mezz.) French Sculptures - Oriental Antiquities 🚻 6-16
FIRST FLOOR   Objets d'Art Napoleon 111 Apartments 🚻 26-86
SECOND FLOOR   Paintings French, Dutch, Flemish and German 🚻 19

Mons, Weds, Thurs, Fris, Sats, Suns. 09.00 - 18.00 Closed Tuesday. Wednesdays all departments close at 21.45. Under 18s free first Sunday of the month. Reduced rate after 15.00.   *Charge*

NOTRE-DAME

See Map 40 Square C3

Paris dawned on the 'Île de la Cité' and on this site nearly 2000 years ago Gallic and Roman gods were worshipped in a Temple of Jupiter. With the arrival of Christianity, a church was built in 365. Later, in the 6th century, this was replaced by a cathedral; it was at the time the largest church in Gaul. To get some idea of the size, you can see the outline of the walls on the parvis of Notre-Dame. The cathedral was later detroyed by Norman raiders. Two other romanesque churches followed, and then Maurice de Sully, the Bishop of Paris, demolished them. In 1163 he started to build the magnificent Gothic cathedral we see today. It was not until 1250 that the towers were completed. The flying buttresses, beautifully constructed, were 14th century additions to the apse (an original feature).

During the Revolution, when it was renamed 'The Temple of Reason', many sculptures and statues were destroyed and replaced, in some cases, by images of Voltaire and Rousseau. On the facade of the building, the Kings of Israel and Judea were pulled down - the people mistook them for their own monarchs.

In need of great repair until returned to its former glory by Napoleon Bonaparte, the cathedral that had witnessed the crowning of an English monarch Henry VI at the time of the 100 Years War witnessed one of its most impressive occasions - the crowning of Napoleon by the Pope. This event is depicted in Louis David's great painting of the Coronation, which can be seen in the Louvre.

By the mid 19th century, Viollet le Duc and his master craftsmen were restoring the cathedral. The spire that had been taken down half a century before, because of increasing decay, was skilfully reconstructed. Leading up to the base of the spire from four sides are the Apostles and Evangelists made in copper - now turned green. As is customary one of the craftsmen has used the boss as a model: his effigy, with elbow raised is at the SE angle. The best view and the most thought provoking in Paris can be seen from the top of Notre-Dame. It is worth climbing the 385 steps! Ascend by the North Tower, cross over to the South Tower, then make the decision whether to go to the top or descend. When you cross over the open gallery, you can see: Viollet le Duc's effigy, and many of his creations, the gargoyles (which disperse the rainwater) carved beasts, griffins, demons, and birds. The South Tower also houses 'Le Gros Bourdon', the great 13 ton bell that dates from the 15th century. Recast and named Emmanuel in Louis XIV's reign in 1683, it is pitched in F sharp.

The Quai de Montebello offers the best prospect for photographs of the intricate architectural detail of the cathedral. From the parvis you see the front only, with the Kings ranged over the three portals. In medieval times the original statues were painted. The Virgin and Child between two angels are in front of the Rose window, and on the same level on each tower respectively are Adam and Eve.

When entering the Cathedral you stand beneath France's largest organ. Originally 14th century, the casing dates from 1731, and has been reconstructed over the years. The organ is now electrified, and has a computer which links over 7500 pipes. In the transept is the statue of Mary. Although not the original, this statue dates back to the 14th century. This is also the position to view the rose windows;

the north one contains a great deal of the original medieval glass.

Located at the far end of the parvis (C3 40) is the Crypte Archéologique. In the crypt are remains of buildings and walls built on the site from Gallo - Roman times onwards.

Crypte open daily except Tuesday 10.00-16.30 Charge
Museum, 10 rue de Cloître.   C3 40
Open Weds, Saturday and Sunday 14.30-18.00 Charge
Treasury Monday - Saturday 14.00-18. 00 Charge
Cathedral *open every day 08.00-16.30*   *Free*
Towers *closed Tuesday, open 10.00-16.30   Charge*

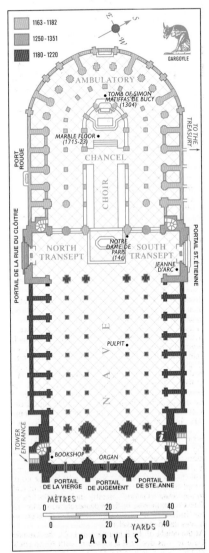

MUSEUMS AND ART GALLERIES

ARMÉE. MUSÉE DE L' B2 38
Esplanade des Invalides, 75007. The 'Hotel des Invalides', built by Louis XIV in 1676, was once a hospital for war veterans. Today it contains a remarkable collection of French and international military regalia, including uniforms, weapons, armour and flags dating from the Middle Ages to the Second World War. You will also find many models and a great deal of memorabilia that relate to Napoleon Bonaparte.
Napoleon's Tomb. In Les Invalides there are two interconnected churches, St.Louis - the soldiers church - and the Église du Dome (1706). The latter contains the sarcophagus of Napoleon - six coffins placed inside each other. This is situated directly underneath the great golden dome.
Daily 10.00 -18.00 April to September
October to March 10.00 - 17.00   *Charge*

ART MODERNE. MUSÉE D' F5 29
de la Ville de Paris 11 Av. Pres. Wilson, 75016 Built for the 1937 World Fair, the Palais de Tokyo holds a collection of paintings of Cubists, fauvists, and members of the Paris school including murals by Delaunay, Bracque, Matisse, and Raoul Dufy's huge 'Fée Electricité'.
Tuesday to Sunday 10. 00 - 17. 40 (Wednesday 20.30)
Closed Monday   *Charge*

BOURDELLE. MUSÉE ANTOINE C1 44
16 Rue Antoine Bourdelle, 75015. This museum in Montparnasse, is built around the sculptor's studio where he worked until his death in 1929. On view are bronzes, granites, marbles, paintings and drawings, and his preparatory work for the Théâtre des Champs-Élysees. All superbly displayed.
Tuesday to Sunday 10.00 - 17. 40   *Charge*

CARNAVALET. MUSÉE F2 41
23 Rue de Sévigné, 75003. Situated in the Marais district, the 16th century mansion is one of the most interesting of the Paris museums. It illustrates the history and development of Paris up to the present day, by using 'Objets d'Art'. Well worth a visit.
Tuesday to Sunday 10.00 - 17.40   *Charge*

CENTRE GEORGES POMPIDOU D6 32
Musee National d'Art Moderne, 75004.
This museum, behind all the exterior piping, boasts one of the finest permanent collections of contemporary art in the world, and brings together all forms of plastic arts. Cubism, fauvism, surrealism, abstracts and pop art and new realism are all exhibited in this building.
Weekdays 12.00 - 22.00,
Sats and Suns 10.00 - 22.00. Closed Tuesday Charge

CERNUSCHI. MUSÉE B5 22
7 Av. Vélasquez, 75008. Close to the Parc Monceau the museum exhibits ancient and contemporary Chinese art: neolithic pottery, archaic bronzes and funerary statues from as early as 300 BC.
Tues to Suns 10.00 - 17.40. Closed Monday Charge

CITÉ DES SCIENCES E1 27
30 Rue de Corentin Cariou, 75019. In the cultural complex of La Villette (Métro Porte de la Villette) is the largest technical and scientific museum in Europe, researching the present and the future of mankind. There are discovery areas for children, a planetarium, aquarium, cinema, displays of light and sound, biology, and 'the secrets of life'. Outside and unmistakable is the Géode, which contains an auditorium with a 180 degree hemispheric screen.
Tues, Thurs, and Fris 10.00-18.00, Weds 12.00-21.00
Closed Mons.Weekend and Hols 12.00-20.00 Charge

CLUNY. THERMES DE B4 40
6 Pl. Paul Painlevé, 75005.   The remains of the Roman baths of Lutetia adjoin the Hôtel de Cluny - a 15th century town residence once occupied by abbots. The museum is renowned for the 'Lady with Unicorn' tapestries, and the Kings of Judea sculptures from the facade of Notre-Dame. It also features a collection of Medieval arts and crafts.
Wednesday to Monday 09.30 - 17.15   *Charge*

COGNACQ-JAY. MUSÉE F1 41
8 Rue de Elzévir, 75003. In the heart of the Marais district the museum is named after the founders of the Samaritaine stores, whose collection of 18th century art was bequeathed to the city. It includes porcelain, furniture, sculpture and paintings, with works by Watteau, Canaletto, and Rembrandt.
Tuesday to Sunday 10.00 - 17.40   *Charge*

DÉCOUVERTE. PALAIS DE LA A4 30
Av. F.D.Roosevelt, 75008. The west wing of the Grand Palais, just off the Champs-Élysées, houses the Discovery museum, where you can watch, and often participate in, various scientific experiments. Another feature of this museum is the planetarium.
Tues to Sat 09.30 - 18.00. Suns 10.00 - 19.00 Charge

EDITH PIAF. MUSÉE C4 34
5 Rue Crespin du Gast, 75011. In a quiet street in Ménilmontant on the 4th floor of a block of flats is a small private museum, dedicated to the life of one of the world's great entertainers, Edith Piaf. The flat is not far from Père Lachaise cemetery 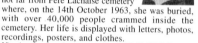 where, on the 14th October 1963, she was buried, with over 40,000 people crammed inside the cemetery. Her life is displayed with letters, photos, recordings, posters, and clothes.
Viewing by appointment. ☎ *43 55 52 72 Voluntary*

EUGÉNE DELACROIX. MUSÉE G3 39
6 Rue de Furstemberg, 75006. The last home of the great 19th century painter (1798-1863) is situated behind the church of St.Germain. The museum features paintings and personal posessions.
Weds to Mons 09.45-12.30 and 14.00-17.15 Charge

GUIMET. MUSÉE E4 29
6 Pl. d'Iéna, 75116. This museum is devoted to the art of Asia, with all the richness and diversity of the region's different cultures. Outstanding are the collections of Chinese porcelain, Khmer sculptures, and Tibetan paintings on canvas. Two galleries depict the Buddhist pantheon of China and Japan, and are a feature of this museum.
Wednesday to Monday 09.45 - 17.15   *Charge*

GRÉVIN. MUSÉE A2 32
10 Bd. Montmartre, 75009. The wax museum of Paris on the Grands Boulevards contains over 500 wax figures depicting the history of France up to the present day. There is also an annexe in Les Halles (B2 32) which brings to life the early 1900s 'Belle Epoque' era in Paris - with tableaux on theatre, fashion and literature with commentary and light.
Daily 13.00 - 19.00, Les Halles 10.30 -19.30 Charge

GUSTAVE MOREAU. MUSÉE G5 23
14 Rue de la Rochefoucauld, 75009. Not far from Pigalle is the house and studio of symbolist artist Gustave Moreau (1826-98). He painted classical and religious subjects, and is recognised as the source of surrealism. Many watercolours and oil paintings including his famous 'L'Apparition' can be viewed.
Weds to Mons 11.00 - 12.45, 14.00 - 17.15 Charge

INSTITUT DU MONDE ARABE E5 41
223 Quai St.Bernard, 75005. Close by the Seine on the Left Bank is the Museum of Islamic Art and Civilisation, a modern (1987) building of steel and glass, with a restaurant on the top floor where one can view the panorama of Paris. Displays of glass, carvings, illuminated manuscripts etc. Videotheque.
Tuesday to Sunday 13.00 - 20.00 *Charge*

JACQUEMART-ANDRÉ. MUSÉE A1 30
158 Bd. Haussmann, 75008. An elegant 19th century mansion with fine furniture, Venetian ceilings, bequeathed with all its artworks by banker Edouard André and his wife. This principally 18th century collection includes works by Chardin, Fragonard, Guardi, Franz Hals, Rembrandt, and Reynolds.
Wednesday to Sunday 13.30 - 17.30 *Charge*

MODE ET DU COSTUME. MUSÉE DE LA F4 29
10 Av. Pierre 1er de Serbie, 75016. The Palais Galliera holds temporary exhibitions shown in series from the 18th century to the present day.
See press, Pariscope, for details.
Tuesday to Sunday 10.00 - 17.40 *Charge*

MODE. MUSÉE DES ARTS DE LA G5 31
111 Rue de Rivoli, 75001 This is the fashion museum in the Marsan Pavilion of the Louvre. It holds a large collection of materials and costumes. The exhibitions are temporary - usually six months.

Musee des Arts Décoratifs Adjoining in the same pavilion, this museum depicts the French home from the Middle Ages to the present, with furnished interiors by great designers like Hector Guimard.
Both museums Wednesday to Saturday 12.30-18.00
Sundays 11.00 - 18.00 *Charge*

ORANGERIE. MUSÉE DE L' D5 30
Pl. de la Concorde, 75001. On the south side of the Tuileries Gardens is this gallery renowned for its two rooms displaying Claude Monet's astonishing 'Water Lilies'. Other artists in this collection are Cézanne, Renoir, Matisse, Picasso, Derain etc.
Wednesday to Monday 09.45 - 17.15 *Charge*

ORSAY. MUSÉE D' E1 39
1 Rue de Bellechasse, 75007. Formerly a railway station and hotel built for the Great Exhibition of 1900, this huge steel and glass pavilion once spanned ten platforms. Internally redesigned, it is now a well planned museum displaying artworks from the second half of the 19th to the early 20th centuries. On the ground floor you will find decorative arts, paintings and sculpture from 1850-1870. At the far end of this hall is an interesting architectural section containing models of the Paris Opéra Garnier. Proceed to the upper level for the highlight of the museum, the impressionists and neo-impressionists (from 1870): Monet, Renoir, Pissaro, Sisley, Degas, Manet. Finally descend to the middle level with sculpture of the Third Republic, painting from 1880 onward Bonnard, Vuillard, Roussel; Art Nouveau, with Guimard and Gallé. This floor also contains an exhibition concerned with the 'Birth of the Film Makers'. Behind the extremely photogenic clock is a very elegant restaurant.
Tues,Weds, Fris, Sats 10.00 - 18.00 *Charge*
Thursday 10.00 - 21.45. Sundays 09.00 - 18.00
Opens 09.00 between June 20th and September 20th

CARTE MUSÉES ET MONUMENTS This card is available for one, three or five consecutive days and can be bought in advance and used at any time - the number of visits is unlimited. It allows you to go straight in, often avoiding a queue. Remember, many museums are closed either Monday or Tuesday, so plan carefully.
The Card is available from main Métro Stations, Museums and the Paris Tourist Office.

PALAIS DE CHAILLOT C5 28
Pl. de Trocadéro, 75016. Built for the 1937 fair, the building is divided into two pavilions with a terrace in between. From the terrace visitors experience a superb view looking towards the Eiffel Tower over fountains, gardens and the river Seine. The Palais now holds a National Theatre and four museums:

Musée du Cinéma - Henri Langlois From the 'Magic Lantern' onwards - the thrill of the cinema. Costumes worn by Greta Garbo, Rudolf Valentino; model sets by Eisenstein; posters, cameras and screenings of important films every day.
Guided Visits in French (90 mins. duration) 10.00,
11.00, 14.00, 15.00, 16.00. Closed Tuesday Charge

Musée de l'Homme The anthropological museum that shows the evolution of man from pre-history, illustrating the various world cultures by dividing the earth into sections.
Wednesday to Monday 09.45 - 17.15 *Charge*

Musée de la Marine French naval history from the 17th century to the present day, with many superb models of ships, charts, instruments and associated works of maritime art.
Wednesday to Monday 10.00 - 18.00 *Charge*

Musée National des Monuments Français Copies and mouldings of wall decorations, sculpture and carvings from the great churches of France. With some audio visual presentation.
Wednesday to Monday 09.00 -18.00 *Charge*

PETIT PALAIS. MUSÉE DU B4 30
Av. Winston-Churchill, 75008. Facing the Grand Palais, this building was also erected for the exhibition of 1900. It is a fine-arts museum, and the exhibits range from ancient times to the 20th century. Its rich collection includes: sculptures, tapestries, furniture and objets d'art. The paintings include works by Cézanne, Courbet and Monet.
Tuesday to Sunday 10.00 - 17.40 *Charge*

PICASSO. MUSÉE F1 41

VIOLIN

5 Rue de Thorigny, 75003. This is Picasso's private collection in the Hôtel de Salé in the Marais district. Every period of his life work can be seen displayed in very sympathetically decorated surroundings. Paintings by other artists and friends are also on view. *Thursday to Monday 12.00 - 18.00. Closed Tuesday Sunday 09.30 -18.00* *Charge*

RODIN. MUSÉE AUGUSTE C2 28
77 Rue de Varenne, 75007. The Hôtel Biron, a small, beautiful 18th century mansion with a large garden, once the home of several artists including Rodin, the sculptor, whose works are displayed in the house and garden. Rodin, the creator of 'The Thinker' and the 'Burghers of Calais', lived here from 1908 until his death in 1917.
Daily October to March 10.00 - 17.00
April to Sept 10.00 - 17.45. Closed Mons *Charge*

OTHER MUSEUMS

B2 36	Maison de Balzac	Author's House
A2 38	Musée de la Contrefaçon	Counterfeiting
D1 32	Musée du Cristal	Glass Crystal
B2 28	Musée d'Ennery	Objets d'Art,China-Japan
D5 38	Musée Hebert	Paintings and Drawings
H4 21	Musée Henner	Paintings and Drawings
H2 23	L'Historial	Wax Museum
D6 32	Instruments de Musique Mécanique	
B5 22	Musée Nissim de Camondo	18c Home
C2 44	Musée de la Poste	Philately
G4 23	Musée Renan Scheffer	Georges Sand
F5 41	Musée de la Sculpture en Plein Air	
A2 24	Musée du Vieux Montmartre	
G1 45	Musée Zadkine	Sculptor's Workshop

ARC DE TRIOMPHE   E1 29
P1. Charles de Gaulle, 75008. One of the best known
landmarks of Paris, commissioned by Napoleon in
1806, to honour his armies. It was designed by
Chalgrin in the style of the great Roman arches and
was not completed until 1836 (Napoleon died in
1821). Of the four lower relief sculptures, the one
facing the Champs-Élysées on the right, called the
'Marseillaise' by François Rude, is considered the
best. The arch is 50 metres high and 45 metres wide.
Climb the stairs or take the lift to the top: from here
you can see the twelve avenues radiating outwards;
a fine view of Paris and the Bois de Boulogne.
Directly under the Arc lies the 'Tomb of the
Unknown Warrior'. Every evening at 18.30 a small
commemoration ceremony is held.
Daily 10.00 - 17.30. Winter 16.30   *Charge*

ARÈNES DE LUTÈCE   D6 40
47 Rue Monge, 75005. The remains of a 1st century
Roman amphitheatre, unearthed in 1869. The arena
once held over 15,000 spectators. Today it is a
popular place for the french pastime of boules. A
nice place to watch, sit, rest, eat sandwiches or just
contemplate history.
Daily Summer 10.00 - 20.30 (Winter 17.30)   *Free*

BIBLIOTHÈQUE NATIONALE   H4 31
58 rue de Richelieu, 75002. One of the richest
libraries in the world. The original mansion is 17th
century, with the magnificent vaulted iron and glass
roof of the reading room added between 1857 and
1868. The library holds manuscripts, music, maps,
coins, medals and antiques.
Closed to the general public; temporary exhibitions
allow you a chance to peep at the architecture.
The new Bibliothèque Nationale François Mitterand
(B5 48) at Tolbiac holds the sound archives as well
as over ten million books and periodicals.

CATACOMBES. LES   G5 45
1 P1. Denfert.Rochereau, 75014.   Not places of
prayer like the catacombs in Rome, but a network
of disused limestone quarries, containing neat piles
of skulls and bones taken from Parisian graveyards.
The tunnels are not very well lit, so take a torch.
Monday to Friday14.00 - 16.00   *Charge*
Saturday and Sunday 09.00 - 11.00, 14.00 - 16.00

CEMETERIES

Cimetière de Montmartre   F2 23
20 Av. Rachel, 75018. The cemetery dates back to
1797, and contains the graves of Berlioz, Dégas,
Delibes, Émile Zola, Offenbach, Sacha Guitry,
Alexandre Dumas the Younger, Alphonsine Plessis
(the Lady of the Camelias), Nijinsky and Richard-
a more recent addition - who is he?

Cimetière du Montparnasse   E3 45

3 Bd. Edgar-Quinet, 75014. The last
resting place of Baudelaire, Maupassant,
Alfred Dreyfus, Jean Seberg, Jean-Paul
Sartre (with Simone de Beauvoir next to
him), and Marie Montez, the cult screen
idol of the 40s (Mrs Jean-Pierre Aumont).
In a corner of the cemetery (see map),
and well worth viewing is the joyously
simple gravestone called'The Kiss', by the Romanian
sculptor Constantin Brancusi: he is also buried in
this cemetery.

Cimetière de Passy   C5 28
Place du Trocadéro, 75016. A small cemetery
situated close by the Palais de Chaillot, where
Debussy, Fernandel, Manet and Fauré all rest.

Cimetière de Père-Lachaise   E6 35
Bd. de Ménilmontant, 75020. One of the most
celebrated burial places in th world. It was here, in
1871, that the 147 survivors of the Commune were
stood against the wall, Mur des Fédérés, and shot.

Together lie such famous spirits as: Modigliani,
Bizet, Seurat, Balzac, Colette, Proust, Gertrude
Stein,Oscar Wilde (the elongated sculpted figure by
Epstein is unfortunately impaired), Chopin, Simone
Signoret, and the 'little sparrow', Edith Piaf, by the
side of her last husband, Théo Sarapo. Always a site
to see is the grave of spiritualist Allan Kardec, which
is usually massed with flowers. You also cannot fail
to see graffiti signs all over the cemetery, which lead
you to the grave of rock star Jim Morrison.
16th March to 5th November 07.30 - 18.00
Winter 08.00 - 17.30. Sundays from 09.30

CONCIERGERIE. LA   B2 40
Île de la Cité, 75001. A part of the old Royal Palace
dating from 1268-1314. Later it was to become
the supreme court and finally a prison under the
concierge's jurisdiction. Many famous people were
imprisoned here during the Revolution: Marie
Antoinette (whose cell can be viewed), Robespierre
and the poet André Chénier were among thousands
who awaited the guillotine. The building has
tremendous atmosphere and is well worth a visit.
The Hall of the Men at Arms, the Hall of the Guards,
with their mass of Gothic vaulting, and the huge
kitchens with their huge fireplaces all 'take you back
in time'. Outside on the north-east tower, Tour de
l'Horloge, is a magnificent clock, the first public one
in Paris, dating from 1585.
Daily 10.00 - 16.30
April to September 10.00 - 17.30   *Charge*

ÉCOLE MILITAIRE   H4 37
Av. de la Motte-Picquet, 75007. A fine example of
18th century neo-classical architecture at the south
end of the Champs de Mars gardens. It is still used
by the army as an officers training college; its most
famous student was young Napoleon!

EIFFEL TOUR   E1 37
Pont d'Iéna, 75007.   The symbol of Paris and a
monument to the engineer Gustave Eiffel. Erected
for the exposition of 1889, it was assembled by 210
men in 21 months. The tower, originally 300 metres
high (now 320m) has an iron framework supported
by four masonry piers. There are three platforms;
the first and second have a restaurant, bars and shops.
From the top stage you can see over 50 miles
on a clear day. It does get very crowded and there
is often a long wait to go up and come down. The
best time to view is an hour before sunset.
Daily 10.00 to 23.00   *Charge*

FORUM DES HALLES   B6 32
Les Halles, 75001. On the site where the foodmarket
once stood you will find a garden, around which are
many cafes, shops, jazz clubs and the beautiful
St.Eustache church. Free of traffic, young people
have chosen this area to sit and play their music,
while others glide around on skate-boards. The focal
point and meeting place is by the 'Fontaine des
Innocents', which dates back to 1549.
Underneath all the greenery is a vast shopping,
entertainment and sports centre, with a large Metro
station. The Forum includes a swimming pool,
gymnasium, wax museum, holography museum,
shops, cafes, an auditorium, library, theatres, cinemas
and the Parc Océanique Cousteau- an underwater
world without water!

GRANDE ARCHE de la DÉFENSE see Métro map
Built in the business district of La Défense in 1989,
and aligned on a course running from the Louvre
through the Arc de Triomphe. Panoramic view.
Suns to Thurs 09.00-17.00. July, August 10.00-19.00
Fris, Sats 10.00-19.00. July, August 21.00 Charge

GRAND PALAIS B4 30

3 Av.du Gén.Eisenhower, 75008 An impressive fronted building with colonnades and statues, close to the trees, off the Champs-Élysées. This neo-baroque structure with its long vaulted steel and glass roof was built, like the Petit Palais across the road, for the Exposition Universelle of 1900. Part of the building is taken up with the scientific Discovery Museum, while the rest is always exhibiting some of the best temporary art displays in Paris.
See press for details.
Thurs to Tues 10.00-20.00, Wednesday 21.15 Charge

HÔTEL DES MONNAIES H2 39

11 Quai de Conti, 75006. Across the Seine from the Louvre on the Left Bank is the old 18th century Royal Mint, commissioned by Louis XV. The long frontage (118m) overlooks the equestrian statue of Henri IV on the Île de la Cité. Inside, a museum has been created to tell the history of France, using coins and medals. There is also a shop, and a workshop producing medals to order. *Tuesday and Friday 14.15 - 18.00 Thurs, Sat, Sun 13.00 - 18.00, Weds 21.00 Charge*

HÔTEL DE SENS E3 41

1 Rue de Figuier, 75004. A medieval Gothic building dating from 1474 with cylindrical turrets, battlements and gables, once the residence of the Archbishop of Sens. It is also one of the oldest buildings in Paris. A home to archbishops and royalty, the mansion fell into disrepair and was diversely used as a stage coach terminus for the Paris-Bourgogne route, and as a jam factory. Before the First World War it had become a manufactory for glass. Today, it has been restored and it now contains the Forney Library, which specialises in science and applied arts. It also holds a collection of posters and wallpaper.
Temporary exhibitions are held here.
Tuesday to Saturday 13.30 - 20.30

HÔTEL DE VILLE D2 40

29 Rue de Rivoli, 75004. Since 1357 there has been a Town Hall on this site. It all began with the powerful Boatmen's Guild who gave their arms to the city of Paris (see Page 4). The first purpose-built Town Hall was constructed between 1533 and 1628, then later, in 1835, two wings were added on each side looking from the parvis. The Communards, who were facing defeat in 1871, set fire to it. After the insurrection was crushed, it was rebuilt, very much as it was before, in the Renaissance style. On the facade are many statues of the famous. The interior is renowned for its sumptuous rooms and decorations. Guided Tours Mondays 10.30 *Charge*

JARDIN DES PLANTES F6 41

57 Rue Cuvier, 75005. The Botanical Gardens of Paris, founded by Louis XII to cultivate medicinal plants, now contain over 10,000 species of plants. Also in the gardens are a small zoo, an alpine garden, the trunk of a 2000-year-old sequoia tree dated with historic events, and the Museum of Natural History, which houses prehistoric skeletons and fossils illustrating the evolution of animal and plant life.
Gardens *Daily 08.00 - 17.00 Free*
Zoo *Daily 09.00 - 17.00 Charge*
Museum *10.00-17.00, Closed Tues, Bank Hols Charge*

MONTPARNASSE. TOUR D2 44

33 Av. du Maine, 75015. From the 56th and the 59th floors a complete view of Paris in all directions can be seen. It has an open air roof terrace, shops and a restaurant. Without the panache of the Eiffel Tower and usually no queues and not as crowded.
Daily Oct-Mar 10.00-21.00, April-Sept 09.0-23.00 Charge. Restaurant on 56th floor midday to 02.00

L'OBSERVATOIRE H$ 45

61 Av. de l'Observatoire, 75014. The Observatory was built in 1672 with the outside walls facing the cardinal points of the compass. Iron was not used in the construction in order not to upset the delicate balance of the instruments. At one time, for the purpose of French map-making, 0 degree longitude ran through the building: since 1911 the Greenwich meridian has been accepted by France.

PALAIS ROYAL H5 31

Place du Palais Royal, 75001. Although in the centre of the business district, this is a calm haven away from the bustle. Once the residence of Cardinal Richelieu, this lovely Palace was built in 1639, the arcaded gardens were added in the 18th century. It was here that Camille Desmoulins incited the Revolution. Today, you can wander round the interesting shops in the arcade or sit at a café table.

PANTHÉON B6 40

Place du Panthéon, 75005. A majestic neo-classical monument, in former years it was the church of Ste. Geneviève; it became a mausoleum in 1791. The motto engraved across its pediment reads: 'To her Great Men, from Grateful France'. Rousseau, Voltaire, Victor Hugo, and Émile Zola are buried here. In 2001 the remains of Marie Curie and her husband Pierre were removed to the resting place of great men!
April to September 10.00-17.30, October to March 10.00-12. 00, 14.00-17.30 Charge

PLACE DE LA CONCORDE B6 40

The centre of French history from the Revolution onwards. If you brave the traffic and stand in the centre, close by the 3rd century BC Egyptian obelisk of Luxor, planted here in 1833, on all sides you have superb vistas of the Tuileries, Arc de Triomphe, Madeleine and the Palais Bourbon. You are also not far from where the guillotine was erected. On their sentry boxes are eight statues representing cities of France, and guarding the entrance to the Champs Élysées are the superb Marly horses. The floodlit fountains are also a sight to behold.

PLACE DES VOSGES G2 41

75004. Close to the Place de la Bastille in the SE part of the Marais district is this peaceful old world square. With a railed garden framed by 36 pavilions, the Place was built two storeys high above arcades. Originally called Place Royale when it was built in 1615, it is the oldest square in Paris. Many famous people have lived here. At number six on the south side, the author of 'Les Miserables', Victor Hugo lived. Today, it is a museum venerating him, crowded with paintings, photographs, mementoes, and his own drawings. It is a little known fact that he was also an exceptional artist.
Museum *10.00-17.40 closed on Monday Charge*

ST. JACQUES. TOUR C1 40

Rue de Rivoli, 75004. Formerly the bell-tower of a 16th century Gothic church, the tower had a preservation order on it when the church was auctioned and demolished in 1797. Today, it is used as a meteorological station. Beneath the tower there stands a statue of Blaise Pascal, the mathematician and theologian, who experimented here on the weight of air.

OTHER PLACES OF INTEREST ON THE MAPS

G5 29 Les Égouts - The entrance to the sewers.
D4 46 Manufacture des Gobelins - A traditional carpet and tapestry factory.
C6 30 Palais Bourbon - 1722-28 the residence of the Lower House of Parliament.
D3 32 Porte St. Denis - Triumphal Arch 1672, designed by François Blondel
E3 36 Porte St. Martin - Triumphal Arch 1674
A4 36 Statue of Liberty - A smaller version of the original which stands in Upper New York Bay.

CHURCHES OF INTEREST

1st Arrondissement

SAINTE CHAPELLE — B4 20
Small and exquisite, this private chapel, full of light and colour, was built by Louis IX and is well worth visiting. A popular saying about wine is: 'It was tinted like the stained glass of the Ste.Chapelle', and you can understand why. Most of the glass of the slender vaulted upper chapel is still 13th century: about a third is part of the 19th century renovation.
10.00 - 17.30 — *Charge*

ST. EUSTACHE — B5 32
Above the Les Halles shopping centre. Finished in 1637, it is the largest Renaissance church in France, and contains one of the finest organs in Paris. Renowned for its music, choir, and concerts.

5th Arrondissement

ÉGLISE DE LA SORBONNE — B5 50
The Sorbonne is the most famous university in Paris, and was founded in the Middle Ages. The Romanesque style church is the oldest standing part of the University, and dates back to 1642. Inside is the tomb of Cardinal Richelieu, who commissioned Jacques Le Mercier to build the church. The classic facade is extremely impressive when it is viewed from the courtyard, where the three levels and Corinthian columned portico are clearly visible.

ST.ÉTIENNE DU MONT — C6 40
Started in 1492 and completed by 1626, it is an amalgam of styles. The frontage has a strange, three level pediment, behind which is a bell tower, with an enclosed spiral staircase on the outside. Many of the windows contain 16th-17th century stained glass,but the most striking feature is the rood screen, with two spiral staircases on each side. There is nothing else like it in Paris! Look out for the sculpted figure of Samson supporting the (1650) pulpit. This is Ste.Geneviève's church and her sarcophagus and relics are held here. Two great men also lie beneath the church: Pascal and Racine.

ST. SÉVERIN — B4 40
In the heart of the Latin Quarter is this old Gothic university church. Behind the altar is an amazing flamboyant ambulatory, described as 'a forest of pine trees'. It has a contemporary window by Jean Bazaine (1970) in seven different colours. Other windows date back to the late 15th century.

VAL DE GRÂCE — A2 46
A fine church completed in 1667, with a baroque style interior featuring a dome painted in fresco by Pierre Mignard in 1664.

6th Arrondissement

ST. GERMAIN DES PRÉS — G3 39

Across the road from the great cafés stands the oldest church in Paris, on the site of a 6th century monastery. This Romanesque style church has an 11th century bell tower and nave; in the chancel are marble columns taken from the earlier 6th century basilica. The Abbots' Palace (1590), next to it, is the only other part of the monastery remaining. In the garden on the NW corner is a Picasso sculpture dedicated to the poet Apollinaire.

ST.SULPICE — G4 39
With an interior larger than Notre-Dame, it has a monumental west front, facing a fountain (1847) depicting the four cardinal points of the compass, on which are placed four preachers who never became cardinals! The church was completed in 1777 and the towers on either side of the double portico are the work of Chalgrin. You may notice that they are not identical! The transept has inlaid in the floor a copper band meridian, running S to N orientating on an obelisk; sunlight on the line enables the time to be measured throughout the year. There are paintings by Eugène Delacroix and Carlo Van Loo, and a sculpted 'Virgin and Child' by Jean Pigalle.

8th Arrondissement

LA MADELEINE — E3 31
Construction started in 1764 on a church, which was unfinished when the Revolution began. Then in 1806, Napoleon gave instructions for a 'Temple of Glory', dedicated to his armies, to be built on the site. Pierre Vignon was asked to design the outside as a larger version of the 'Maison Carrée' in Nîmes (the most complete example of a Roman temple still standing today). Long before it was finished in 1842, it had been decided that it was to be a church. There had been other suggestions for the building: a bank, theatre and the city's first railway station. Although it is without windows, a small amount of light is admitted through the three oblate cupolas. An imposing building, it has 52 Corinthian columns on a plinth, with a flight of steps leading up to the front portico, and an immense bronze door. From the steps looking towards Concorde, there is a mirror image with the rear colonnades of the Palais Bourbon. Inside it is paved and faced with marble, more opulent than you would expect from the exterior. It has good acoustics and a splendid organ. François Rude's 'The Baptism of Christ' is on the left side of the vestibule.

18th Arrondissement

SACRÉ-CŒUR BASILICA — B2 24
After the Franco - Prussian war and the Commune riots of 1871, when there were artillery batteries positioned on the waste ground on top of the Butte Montmartre, the National Assembly decided by a decree to build an expiatory church on the site. An architect, M.Abadie,was given the job of designing a basilica,in the Romano-Byzantine style, similar to his work on Périgueux Cathedral. Deep foundations were required to hold the enormous structure. It is said if the hill blew away, the church would still be there. Completed in 1914, the basilica with its enduring white stone shines all over Paris; often you get a glimpse of it, perhaps reminding you of a painting you have once seen. This beautiful church is approached by the funicular or by climbing 100 metres of monumental steps. From the parvis, the whole of the Paris basin can be viewed; behind you on each side of the portico are two equestrian statues, Joan of Arc and St.Louis. During summer months, the steps are a gathering place for young people from all over the world, with singing and guitar music everywhere. Once inside the church, you are overwhelmed by Oliver Merson's enormous mosaic depicting Christ wearing a Heart of Gold. From the west wing you can ascend a spiral staircase to the colonnades under the dome for another view of Paris. Le Savoyarde is the name of the huge bell struck in C and accompanied by four others. On leaving the basilica, turn right towards the Place du Tertre where the artists mingle. On your way you will pass the Church of St. Pierre de Montmartre, dating back to the 12th century, on a site where a Roman Temple of Mercury once stood.

LA MOSQUÉE DE PARIS — D2 46
75005. Close by the Jardin des Plantes is the Mosque of Paris. Built in 1926 it is a picturesque collection of moorish courtyards, with a minaret and a patio garden. Guided tours are in French *09.00-12.00,14.00-18.00.Closed Fridays. Charge*

SHOPPING

One of the many pleasures of Paris is undoubtedly shopping - even if you only window shop. The city is filled with boutiques displaying the fact that Paris today is still the centre of world fashion. Walk along the avenue Montaigne (H4 29), or rue du Faubourg St.Honoré (B2 30) and you see the palaces of the great couturiers. The new aspiring designers are mostly clustered close by the place des Victoires (A4 32). More affordable shops are situated in the Marais district (Page 41).On the Left Bank near the rue de Rennes in St. Germain (F4 39) the boutiques range from chic to trendy; Yves St.Laurent has established two boutiques on the charming place St.Sulpice (G4 39). The Opéra district (Page 31) is where you will find the large department stores, and if you take your passport you may be able to claim discount on some purchases. For a gastronomic treat, try Fauchon near the Madeleine (E2 31), a luxurious delicatessen with a cafeteria where you can sample before buying. Almost out of Zenda, and probably the grandest record shop in the world, is the Virgin shop on the Champs-Élysées (H3 29). Theatre and concert tickets can also be obtained here. For low prices and quite reasonable quality, Monoprix, Innovation, and Uniprix are the shops to buy almost anything you will need. They usually have a food supermarket and are dispersed all over Paris. Many are indicated on the maps.

The Department Stores

BHV   **D2 40**
75004. This store is located close by the Hôtel de Ville. It has a good men's clothes section but tends to concentrate on household items. In the basement there is a large DIY department and on the top floor a self service restaurant. Prices are reasonable.

BON MARCHÉ   **E4 39**
75007. Less crowded and my personal favourite is the oldest department store in Paris, founded in 1852. The internal iron structure is attributed to Gustave Eiffel. The best supermarket in Paris, and an excellent restaurant and self service cafeteria.

GALERIES LAFAYETTE   **F1 31**
75009. Built in the Belle Époque period, and essentially a women's fashion house. Under the magnificent stained glass dome (1895) most of the top designers have small in-store boutiques. The top floor has a self service restaurant, while the ground floor is a large air-conditioned perfume emporium. A smaller store is located in the shopping precinct below the Tour Montparnasse (D1 44).

PRINTEMPS   **F1 31**
75009. Classed as a historic monument, it is three buildings joined by walk-ways: La Mode (women's fashion), La Maison (for the house), and behind them Brummel (men's fashion). The building dates from 1865, and also has a stained glass dome (1923) above the Café Flo, on the sixth floor of La Mode. A good view over the rooftops of Paris can be seen from the ninth floor terrace café of La Maison.

SAMARITAINE   **A1 40**
75001. Overlooking the Seine and the oldest bridge in Paris, the Pont Neuf, this store consists of four buildings. The one facing the Seine is Art Nouveau (1906) and has a superb view from the rooftop terrace café. Everything from do-it-yourself to men, woman and children's fashion. Gradually being modernised to hide some of the old structural girders.
All stores are open 09.30-18.30 Monday to Saturday

Antiques

LOUVRE DES ANTIQUAIRES   **H6 31**
2 Pl. du Palais Royal, 75001. World renowned, with over 250 shops on three floors and very luxurious.
Tuesday to Sunday 11.00 - 19.00

VILLAGE SUISSE   **F4 37**
54 Av. de la Motte-Picquet, 75015. The site of the Swiss pavilion of the world exhibition of 1889. Over 50 boutiques with a special emphasis on furniture,paintings and curios.
Thursday to Sunday 10.30 - 19.00

The Markets of Paris

A visit to Paris is not complete without a trip to one of its many markets. You will probably choose the famous flea market of Clignancourt. Not all the best bargains are found here, and it certainly is not the most attractive of the city's markets. The ones that are listed are just a few; most are on the maps, and can be identified by a symbol (see Page 17).

BEAUVAU-ST.ANTOINE   **B5 42**
75012. Food, clothes, bric-à-brac, jewellery etc.
Daily 07.30 - 12.30 Closed Monday

CHAMPS-ÉLYSÉES   **B3 30**
75008. Situated on the north side of the avenue not far from the place Clemenceau, this is the market for philatelists: postage stamps and postcards.
Thursday, Saturday and Sunday until dusk.

CITÉ DES FLEURS   **C2 40**
75004. A much loved market on the Île de la Cité, selling flowers Monday to Saturday. Sunday there is a small animal market: birds, cats and dogs.
Mon-Sat 8.00-19.30. Animal Market Suns 8.00-19.00

MARCHÉ BIOLOGIQUE   **E5 39**
75006. In the centre of the boulevard Raspail, the organic food market of Paris.   *Sunday Mornings*

PUCES DE CLIGNANCOURT   **See Page 24**
75018. Métro Porte de Clignancourt. The largest flea market in Europe. Go early and head for the centre of the market. Almost anything: clothes, leather, antiques, lamps, furniture, records, etc.
Saturday, Sunday and Monday 07.00 - 19.30

PUCES MONTREUIL   Métro Porte de Montreuil
75020. Clothes, furniture, hats, leather etc.
Saturday, Sunday and Monday 07.00 - 19.30

PUCES VANVES   Métro Porte de Vanves
75014. Bric-à-brac, antiquarian books, silver etc. Also a corner where artists sell their paintings.
Saturday, Sunday and Monday 07.00 - 19.30

RUE DE BUCI (Rue de Seine)   **H3 39**
75006. A very small and colourful food market, with two supermarkets and a wine shop close by.
Daily - Shop hours. Closed Mondays.

RUE MOUFFETARD   **C2 46**
75005. The lively and exotic street market of the Latin Quarter - one of the oldest in Paris. In the nearby place Monge (D1 46) there is also a market on Wednesday, Friday and Sunday.

ST. PIERRE   **B3 24**
75018. At the foot of the Sacré-Cœur. Textiles, clothes, shoes.   *Monday to Friday 09.30 - 18.30*

TEMPLE   **F5 33**
75003.   Shops selling new clothes and leather at wholesale prices in a covered market situated very close to the place de la République.
Shops Monday-Saturday 09.00-18.00. Sunday 13.00
Market Daily 09.00-12.30.   Closed Monday

NIGHTLIFE - JAZZ À PARIS

No visitor to Paris should return home without seeing at least just a glimpse of its dazzling nightlife, and there is much to choose from. The glittering cabarets of the Moulin Rouge (G3 23) in Pigalle, the Lido (G2 29) at the top of the Champs-Élysées, and the Paradis Latin (D5 40) on the Left Bank, are just a few to think about. They cater for tours principally, but they do have their points: the Lido has the famous Bluebell girls, and the Moulin Rouge would not live up to its tradition without the Can-Can dancers. The Paradis Latin is, however, more modern, fast and Parisian. Another very similar venue, the Crazy Horse Saloon (G4 29) on the avenue George V, is said to be very expensive and famous for its clientele. Returning to the Left Bank and to St.Germain, the Don Camilo (F2 29) is reputed as having the best food of all the cabaret diners.

Not a cabaret, the Folies Bergère (B1 32) is a very good variety theatre. The shows are fast and have no language barriers! If you want to dine and be waited on by flunkies, the theatre also serves a pre-show candlelit dinner in the vestibule.

Paris caters for all tastes and it should be said that the boulevard de Clichy (G3 23) in Pigalle is the place where an overwhelming choice of cabarets and entertainments are on offer: these should not be confused with the more stylish Moulin Rouge.

Pop concerts are often held in venues like the Palais Omnisports (C3 48) Bercy, or at La Villette (E1 27). The Élysée Montmartre (B4 24) and the Rex cinema (C3 32) hold both rock and jazz concerts.

For the young at heart many discos are located on the maps; by using a listing booklet and the index you may locate them. The longest running disco in Paris (housed in a former Turkish Bath House) is Les Bains (D5 32), it has a Thai restaurant and is off the boulevard de Sébastopol. For a chansonnier, why not try Le Caveau de la République (F3 33)?

On arriving in Paris I would advise you to obtain either Pariscope or L'Officiel des Spectacles. Both magazines are published every week, starting on Wednesday, and are on sale at any news kiosk. The same day Le Figaro prints an entertainment guide.

Paris has always been a haven for black American jazz musicians: even before World War II, many had discovered that Paris treated artists with respect, no matter what nationality or colour they were. Some came and stayed for long periods: Benny Carter, Bill Coleman, Don Byas, Bud Powell and of course Sidney Bechet, who was treated like a king. The cellars of the Left Bank bounced with his rhythm and quivering vibrato! Others, like Charlie Parker and Dizzy Gillespie, came to spread their new music. They took back to America the beret, which became a symbol of early bebop. Today, there are many American musicians, black and white, who frequently sojourn in Paris.

The city also developed during the 1930's its own style of jazz, the 'Hot Club de France', with the gypsy guitar genius of Django Reinhardt and the sonorous toned violin of Stephane Grappelli.

Since I started compiling this Mapguide many clubs have disappeared, only to be replaced by others, confirming that jazz is very much alive in Paris. For serious jazz and listening, the place is the New Morning (D2 32), a converted garage where the great names in jazz have played. If the band or musician is very popular (like the late Stan Getz) it is best to buy your tickets in advance. These can be obtained either from the Virgin Megastore on the Champs-Élysées or any FNAC shop. Many clubs are situated around Les Halles including the Duc des Lombards (C6 32), which is similar to an English pub. On the Left Bank in St.Germain - the district where jazz in France was born - is one of the famous clubs, Le Bilboquet (G3 39) the scene used for the film 'Paris Blues'. This club has a gallery and is a good place to dine and listen. Another club restaurant is Le Petit Journal (A6 40) in St.Michel. If you prefer to dance (jive etc.) or just watch some amazing amateur dancing, then the Slow Club (B1 40) cellar is the place - you cannot miss the neon sign! La Paillote (A5 40) is a bar near l'Odéon that plays jazz CDs and records - a huge mixed selection.

FAMOUS RESTAURANTS CAFÉS AND BARS

As evening approaches, Paris glows, the tables are set and it is time to choose the place to eat. There are so many good restaurants and cafés. You will find your own favourites that you will return to, again and again. Here are a few for a special night out. I have to start with Maxim's (D4 30), immortalised by Franz Léhar and Cole Porter. If you are close to the Garnier Opéra house you might consider the magnificent Belle Epoque Grand Café des Capucines (G2 31). A very expensive but exquisite restaurant, over 200 years old, is Le Grand Véfour (H4 31). This is where Napoléon brought Josephine! On the Left Bank and not so expensive is Le Procope, in the rue de l'Ancienne Comédie H3 39). Outside a plaque proclaims, *'1686, the oldest café in the world'*. Among the list of former clientele are Benjamin Franklin, Voltaire, Danton and Bonaparte. In Montparnasse, La Closerie des Lilas (G2 45) - by Rude's striking statue of Marshal Ney - was frequented by Hemingway and John Dos Passos. Near to the New Morning jazz club is the Brasserie Flo (D2 32), a traditional brasserie with an 1886 interior. In St.Germain the Brasserie Lipp (G3 39) is also well known for its former patrons.

Across the road are two of the most renowned cafés in Paris - Aux Deux Magots and the Café de Flore, which was once almost home to Jean-Paul Sartre and Simone de Beauvoir. In the early 1900's, many of the bohemians moved from Montmartre over the river to Montparnasse, essentially to find cheaper accomodation. Once they settled, the café culture moved with them. The cafés that they frequented became world famous and were featured in many of the novels of that period. To discover some of these haunts, a good starting point is by Rodin's statue of Balzac (F2 45). At the side is La Rotonde, where you could begin by fortifying yourself with some of their great coffee. On the opposite corner is Le Dome. Both the cafés proudly proclaim that Lenin, Trotsky, and Picasso dined there. Further along the boulevard going towards the Tower, you will locate the Select, and opposite, La Coupole, a very large restaurant, with a basement dance floor. Anaïs Nin and Henry Miller dined here when he could afford it.

After a morning in the department stores, walk by the side of the Opéra to the Café de la Paix (F2 31) - Charles Garnier designed the interior of this too.

SERVICES AND USEFUL INFORMATION

Information Centres

OFFICE DE TOURISME WELCOME CENTRES
☎ *(0) 8 92 68 3000*
http://www.paris-touristoffice.com
Carrousel du Louvre *10.00 - 19.00*   Page 6
Eiffel Tower *11.00 - 18.40 (May - Sept.)*   E1 37
Gare du Nord *12.40 - 20.10*   E4 25
Gare de Lyon *8.00 - 18.00 (Mon - Sats)*   A6 42
Opéra *9.00 - 18.30, (Mons-Sats)*   F2 31
Montmartre, Place du Tertre *10.00 -19.00*   A2 24

Emergency Services

POLICE Dial ☎ 17   **FIRE** Dial ☎ 18
AMBULANCE (SAMU) 24 Hour   Dial ☎ 15
MEDICAL SERVICE: DAY   ☎ *(0)1.47.07.77.77*
  NIGHT   ☎ *(0)1.43.37.77.77*
DENTIST 8.00 - 24.00   ☎ *(0)1.43.37.51.00*
ENGLISH HOSPITAL   B1 20
1-3 Rue Barbes, Levallois Perret ☎ *(0)1.47.57.24.10*
AMERICAN HOSPITAL   see A1 20
63 Bd. Victor Hugo, Neuilly   ☎ *(0)1.47.47.53.00*
ALL NIGHT PHARMACY Métro George V **G2 29**
Dhéry, 84 Av. des Champs-Élysées
☎ *(0)1.45.62.02.41*
A few pharmacies open until 01.00. Usual hours are 09.00 - 20.00. Staff are qualified to give advice on minor ailments. See symbol on Page 16.

POST OFFICES PTT offices are open 08.00 - 19.00, Monday to Friday, and 08.00 - 12.00 on Saturday. Stamps and telephone cards can also be obtained at cafés with the TABAC sign. See symbol on Page 16.
24 HOUR POST OFFICE   B5 32
52 Rue de Louvre, 75001.

LOST PROPERTY Métro Porte de Vanves
Bureau des Objets Trouvés, 36 Rue des Morillons, 75015. You will probably have to pay a percentage of the article's value to reclaim it.
Mons -Thurs 8.30 - 19.00, Friday 8.30 - 16.30.

TELEPHONE To make an International call dial 00 then dial the Country Code - United Kingdom 44, USA and Canada 1, Ireland 353, Australia 61, then the Area code followed by the individual number.
NATIONAL HOLIDAYS New Year's Day, Easter Monday, Ascension Day, Victory Day (8th May), Pentecost, Bastille Day (July 14th), Assumption (15th Aug.), All Saints Day (Nov. 1st), Armistice Day (Nov.11th), Christmas Day.
BANKING HOURS Banks open from 09.00 to 16.30 except on Saturdays, Sundays and public holidays. They close at midday before a public holiday.
MÉTRO Public transport in Paris is usually very efficient. The Métro is one of the best underground systems in the world; it was also one of the first. The trains run on rubber wheels and are very quiet and smooth. See map on Pages 2-3: if you wish to travel on line 5 North, follow the signs to the terminus of Bobigny-Pablo Picasso; to go South on line 12 look for the signs to the terminus of Mairie d'Issy. Trains run from 05.30 to approximately 00.30. The 1st Class carriages are only available between 09.00 and 17.00. It is best to buy a pack of 10 tickets - a carnet. Even better is the Coupon Jaune - Carte Orange, which runs from Monday to Sunday, and can be bought in advance at most stations; but first you will need a passport type photo. This card allows unlimited travel on the Métro, buses and RER. You probably will only need Zones 1 and 2 - the Central Area.

BUSES Métro tickets can be used on the buses, when you get on the bus you clip it yourself in the machine (do not clip the Coupon Jaune, just show it). On some journeys you may need more than one ticket for your journey. A glance at the route map displayed on the bus will indicate if another ticket is required. Buses run approximately from 06.30 until 21.00. A few run later, and there are night buses (see the back cover) that run from 01.30 to 05.30.
TAXIS You pay a standard pick up charge plus a metered fare, and a charge for each case or bag. Tipping is 10%. Most taxis take three people only; avoid large taxis as you will pay extra.
Paris Airport Shuttle ☎ *(0) 1.53.10.37.06* run services to the airports and stations with pick-ups from hotels at very reasonable rates.
DISNEYLAND PARIS The RER line A4 runs to a terminus just outside the entrance of Disneyland. Board the train at Châtelet; look for the direction Marne la Vallée. Buy a return ticket and at the other end check the timetable to co-ordinate your return journey. The journey takes about 30 minutes.

Bateaux-Mouches

These luxurious boats with air conditioning and retractable roofs allow you in all weathers, night and day, an unforgettable view of this marvellous city. Trips usually last just over an hour, and have multilingual commentaries. They start in summer at 10.00 and in winter at 11.00. Some operators run cruise restaurants, serving breakfast, tea or dinner.
Full information on these trips is available from:
Bateaux-Mouches (Restaurant)   H5 29
75008. Pont de l'Alma   ☎ *(0)1.42.25.96.10*
Bateaux-Parisiens (Restaurant)   E1 37
75007. Pont d'Iéna   ☎ *(0)1.44.11.33.55*
Vedettes Tour Eiffel (Restaurant)   D1 36
75007. Pont d'Iéna   ☎ *(0)1.45.05.50.00*
Les Vedettes de Paris - Île de France   D2 36
75015 Pont de Bir Hakeim   ☎ *(0)1.47.05.71.29*
Les Vedettes du Pont Neuf   A2 40
75001. Pont Neuf   ☎ *(0)1.46. 33.98.38*

Canal Boat Trips

Canauxrama and Paris Canal run trips on the Canal St. Martin through locks and under the Bastille vault. Trips take about three hours and are usually not as crowded as the river Seine boats. The boats are equipped with telephones, bars and toilets.
Canauxrama ☎ *(0)1.42.39.15.00 Daily 09.15 or 14.30* Port de l'Arsenal to La Villette and vice versa.
Paris Canal ☎ *(0)1.42.40.96.97 Daily 09.30 or 14.00* Musée d'Orsay to La Villette and vice versa.

CLOTHING and SHOE SIZES approximate

SHIRTS							
France	36	37	38	39	40	41	42
UK and USA	14	14.5	15	15.5	16	16.5	17

DRESSES							
France	36	38	40	42	44	46	48
UK	8	10	12	14	16	18	20
USA	6	8	10	12	14	16	18

MEN'S SHOES							
France	39	40	41	42	43	44	45
UK and USA	6	7	7.5	8.5	9	10	11

WOMEN'S SHOES							
France	35.5	36	36.5	37	37.5	38	39
UK	3	3.5	4	4.5	5	5.5	6
USA	4.5	5	5.5	6	6.5	7	7.5

*RER trains from Central Paris to Charles de Gaulle airport are as follows
EMIR - EKLI - EXIL - EBRE. see front of train

16

LEGEND - ENGLISH - FRANÇAIS - DEUTSCH - NEDERLANDS - ITALIANO - ESPAÑOL

HOSPITALS
Hôpitaux
Krankenhäuser
Ziekenhuisen
Ospedali
Hospitales

Hôpital Cochin

POLICE STATION
Gendarmerie
Polizeiwache
Politie
Polizia
Comisaría

G

POST OFFICE
Bureau de Poste
Postamt
Postkantoor
Ufficio Postale
Correos

PHARMACY
Pharmacie
Apotheke
Apotheek
Farmacia
Farmácia

HOTEL
Hôtel
Hotel
Hotel
Albergo
Hotel

HOTEL DES TROIS NATIONS ■

INTERESTING CHURCHES
Églises Intéressants
Sehenswerte Kirchen
Interessant Kirken
Chiese di Interesse
Iglesias de Interes

SAINTE CHAPELLE

SYNAGOGUES
Synagogues
Synagogen
Synagogen
Sinagoghe
Sinagoga

Synagogue ✡

JAZZ CLUB
Jazz Club
Jazz Club
Jazz Club
Jazz Club
Jazz Club

NEW MORNING ★

DISCO or DANCE HALLL
Disco ou Salle de Danse
Disko oder Tanzsaal
Disco of Dans Zaal
Disco o Sala di Danza
Disco o Sala de Danza

La Balajo ★

Metro Station
Station de Métro
U-Bahnstation
Ondergrondse Station
Stazione di Metropolitana
Estación de Metro

Opéra Ⓜ

RER STATION
Station de RER
RER-Station
RER-Station
Stazione di RER
Estación de RER

Auber Ⓡ

TOURIST INFORMATION
Informations Touristiques
Touristenauskünfte
Toeristen Informatie
Informazione Turistiche
Información Turistica

ⓘ

FOOTPATH
Sentier
Fusspfad
Voetpad
Sentiero
Senda

PUBLIC PARK
Jardin Public
Öffentliche Parkanlage
Publiek Park
Giardino Pubblico
Parque Publico

CEMETERY
Cimetière
Friedhöfe
Begraafplaats
Cimiteri
Cementerio

OUTDOOR STATUES and SCULPTURES
Statues et Sculptures dehors
Im Freien stehende Standbilder und Skulpturen
Standbeelden en Beeldhouwkunst buiten
Statue e Sculture all'aperto
Estatura y Escultura al fresco

Jeanne d'Arc •

THEATRES and CONCERT HALLS
Théâtres et Salles de Concerts
Theater und Konzertsäle
Theaters en Concertzalen
Teatri e Sale dei Concerti
Teatros y Salas de Concertos

COMÉDIE FRANÇAIS ■

CINEMA
Cinéma
Kino
Bioscoop
Cinema
Cine

PARAMOUNT OPERA ■

RESTAURANT, CAFE or BAR
Restaurant, Café ou Bar
Restaurant, Cafe oder Bar
Restaurant, Café of Buffet
Ristorante, Cafe o Bar
Restoran, Cafe o Bar

Aux Deux Magots ●

CABARET
Cabaret
Kabarett
Cabaret
Cabaret
Cabaret

CRAZY HORSE SALOON ■

RAILWAY STATION
GARES SNCF
Bahnhöfe der SNCF
SNCF Station
Stazione SNCF
Estaciónes SNCF

SNCF

INTERCHANGE STATION
Station de Correspondance
Umsteigestation
Aansluiting op andere Lijnen
Station di coincidenza
Correspondencia

Ⓜ

🚾 TOILET Toilette Toilet Toeletta Retrete

ARRONDISSEMENTS

See Page 5

8^e

DISTRICT
Arrondissement
Stadibezirke
District
Rione
Distrito

IMPORTANT BUILDINGS
Bâtiments importants
Wichtige Gebäude
Belangrijke gebouwen
Edifici importanti
Edifícios importantes

(TOWN HALL)
MAIRIE
DU VIIe

MUSEUMS, ART GALLERIES and MONUMENTS
Musées et Monuments
Museen und Monumente
Museuma en Gedenkteken
Musei ei Monumenti
Museos y Monumentos

MUSÉE
GUIMET

A SELECTION OF SHOPS
Choix de Magasins
Einige Läden
Keus van Winkels
Scelta di Negozi
Selección de Tiendas

AU
PRINTEMPS

BUS ROUTE TERMINUS
Terminus d'Autobus
Endstation, Autobuslinie
Autobuslijn Eindpunt
Capolinea Autobus
Terminus de Línea Autobús

24

MARKET
Marché
Markt
Markt
Mercato
Mercado

FLEURS M

BUS ROUTES WITH NUMBERS

Ligne d'autobus quotidienne avec numéros - Busstrecke tagsüber mit linien-nummern
Dagelijske Autobuslijn met Nummers - Autobus quotidiano con Numeri
La Ruta de Autobuses durante día con Números

BUS ROUTES in GREY
Arrows indicate BUSES in one direction only.

Lignes d'autobus en GRIS. *Les flèches indiquent les lignes d'autobus dans un seul sens.*

GRAUE busstrecken.
Pfeile zeigen auf Busverkehr nur in Pfeilrichtung.

Autobuslijnen in GRIJS.
Pijlen geven de bussen aan alleen in één direktie.

Linee di Autobus in GRIGIO.
Le frecce indicano autobus in una sola direzione.

Ruta autobús en GRIS.
Las flechas indican la ruta de los autobuses en una sola dirección.

24 72

BUS ROUTE NUMBERS are indicated in the border.

Les lignes dépassant les bordures de la carte sont indiquées en marge.

Buslinien-Nummern sind am Kartenrand angegeben.

Bus route nummers zijn aangegeven in de kantlijn.

I numeri delle linee di autobus son indicate sul margine.

Los números de autobús se indican en el margen.

1:10,000

approximately 6 inches to 1 mile
1 CENTIMETRE TO 100 METRES

SCALE

300 METRES EQUAL 328 YARDS

METRES

0   100   200   300

ENGLISH — The maps are divided into 300 metre squares with divisions of 100 metres indicated in the border.

FRANÇAIS — Les cartes sont divisées en carrés de 300 mètres de côté, avec divisions de 100 mètres indiquées en bordure.

DEUTSCH — Die karten sind in karrees von 300 quadratmeter unterteilt 100-Meter-Unterteilung ist am Rand markiert.

NEDERLANDS — De kaarten zijn verdeeld in vierkanten van 300 meter met verdelingen van 100 meter in de kantlijn.

ITALIANO — Le mappe sono suddivise in 300 metri quadrati con divisione di 100 metri indicate nel margine.

ESPAÑOL — Las cartas están divididas en cuadrados de 300 metros, con divisiones de 100 metros indicados en el margen.

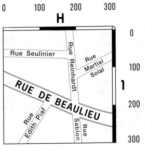

H

0

Rue Seulinier

Rue Reinhardt

Rue Martial Solal

RUE DE BEAULIEU

Rue Edith Piaf

Rue Sablon

100

200

300

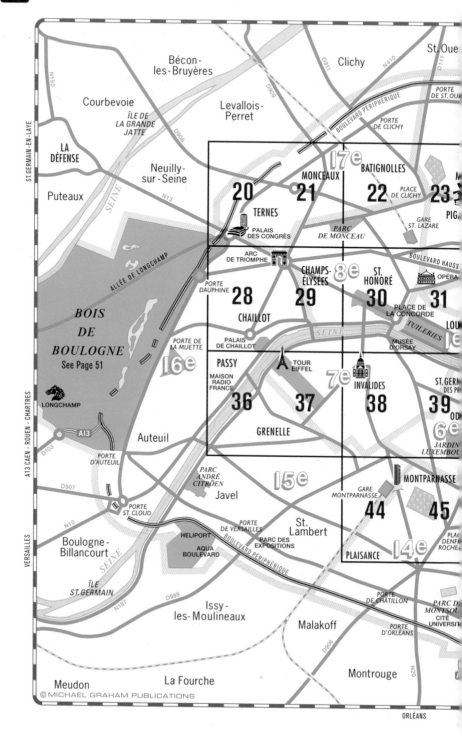

St. Oue
PORTE
DE ST. OUI

Clichy

Bécon-
les-Bruyères

Levallois-
Perret

Courbevoie

ÎLE DE
LA GRANDE
JATTE

BOULEVARD PÉRIPHÉRIQUE

PORTE
DE CLICHY

LA
DÉFENSE

Neuilly-
sur-Seine

17e BATIGNOLLES

MONCEAUX

20 **21** **22** PLACE
DE CLICHY

23

Puteaux

GARE
ST. LAZARE

PIG

TERNES

PALAIS
DES CONGRÈS

PARC
DE MONCEAU

ARC
DE TRIOMPHE

BOULEVARD HAUSS

ALLÉE DE LONGCHAMP

PORTE
DAUPHINE

CHAMPS-
ÉLYSÉES **8e** ST.
HONORÉ

OPÉRA

28 **29** **30** **31**

PLACE DE
LA CONCORDE

BOIS
DE
BOULOGNE
See Page 51

CHAILLOT

PORTE DE
LA MUETTE

PALAIS
DE CHAILLOT

SEINE

TUILERIES

MUSÉE
D'ORSAY

LOU

16e

PASSY

MAISON
RADIO
FRANCE

TOUR
EIFFEL

LONGCHAMP

7e INVALIDES

ST. GERM
DES PI

A13

36 **37** **38** **39**

OD

Auteuil

PORTE
D'AUTEUIL

GRENELLE

6e

JARDIN
LUXEMBOU

PARC
ANDRÉ
CITRÖEN

15e

Javel

GARE
MONTPARNASSE

MONTPARNASSE

PORTE
ST. CLOUD

St.
Lambert

44 **45**

Boulogne-
Billancourt

HELIPORT

PORTE
DE VERSAILLES

PARC DES
EXPOSITIONS

PLAC
DENF
ROCHE

AQUA
BOULEVARD

BOULEVARD PÉRIPHÉRIQUE

PLAISANCE **14e**

ÎLE
ST. GERMAIN

Issy-
les-Moulineaux

PORTE
DE CHÂTILLON

PARC D
MONTSOU
CITÉ
UNIVERSIT

Malakoff

PORTE
D'ORLÉANS

Meudon

La Fourche

Montrouge

ST. GERMAIN-EN-LAYE

A13 CAEN - ROUEN - CHARTRES

VERSAILLES

ORLÉANS

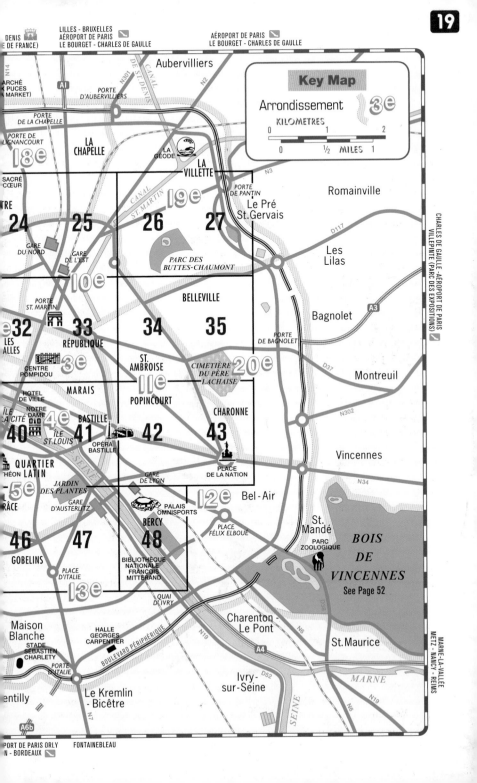

DENIS
(E DE FRANCE)

LILLES - BRUXELLES
AÉROPORT DE PARIS
LE BOURGET - CHARLES DE GAULLE

AÉROPORT DE PARIS
LE BOURGET - CHARLES DE GAULLE

ARCHÉ
K PUCES
A Market)

A1

PORTE
D'AUBERVILLIERS

Aubervilliers

Key Map

Arrondissement **3e**

KILOMETRES
0   1   2

0   ½   MILES   1

PORTE
DE LA CHAPELLE

PORTE DE
LIGNANCOURT

18e

LA
CHAPELLE

LA
GEODE

LA
VILLETTE

PORTE
DE PANTIN

N3

Romainville

SACRÉ
CŒUR

TRE

24

25

26

19e

27

Le Pré
St.Gervais

Les
Lilas

D117

GARE
DU NORD

GARE
DE L'EST

PARC DES
BUTTES-CHAUMONT

10e

PORTE
ST. MARTIN

e**32**

33

34

BELLEVILLE

35

Bagnolet

A3

LES
ALLES

RÉPUBLIQUE

CENTRE
POMPIDOU

3e

ST.
AMBROISE

CIMETIÈRE
DU PÈRE
LACHAISE

20e

PORTE
DE BAGNOLET

D37

Montreuil

HOTEL
DE VILLE

MARAIS

NOTRE
DAME

11e

POPINCOURT

N302

ÎLE
A CITÉ

4e

BASTILLE

CHARONNE

40

ÎLE
ST.LOUIS

41

OPÉRA
BASTILLE

42

43

Vincennes

N34

QUARTIER
HÉON LATIN

5e

JARDIN
DES PLANTES

GARE
DE LYON

PLACE
DE LA NATION

RÂCE

GARE
D'AUSTERLITZ

12e

Bel - Air

St.
Mandé

PALAIS
OMNISPORTS

PLACE
FÉLIX ELBOUÉ

PARC
ZOOLOGIQUE

**BOIS
DE
VINCENNES**
See Page 52

46

GOBELINS

47

BERCY

48

BIBLIOTHÈQUE
NATIONALE
FRANCOIS
MITTERAND

PLACE
D'ITALIE

13e

QUAI
D'IVRY

Charenton -
Le Pont

N6

St.Maurice

Maison
Blanche

HALLE
GEORGES
CARPENTIER

BOULEVARD PÉRIPHÉRIQUE

N19

A4

D52

MARNE

STADE
SEBASTIEN
CHARLETY

PORTE
D'ITALIE

Ivry-
sur-Seine

SEINE

entilly

Le Kremlin
- Bicêtre

N7

N19

N6

A6b

PORT DE PARIS ORLY
N - BORDEAUX

FONTAINEBLEAU

CHARLES DE GAULLE -AÉROPORT DE PARIS
VILLEPINTE (PARC DES EXPOSITIONS)

MARNE-LA-VALLÉE
METZ - NANCY - REIMS

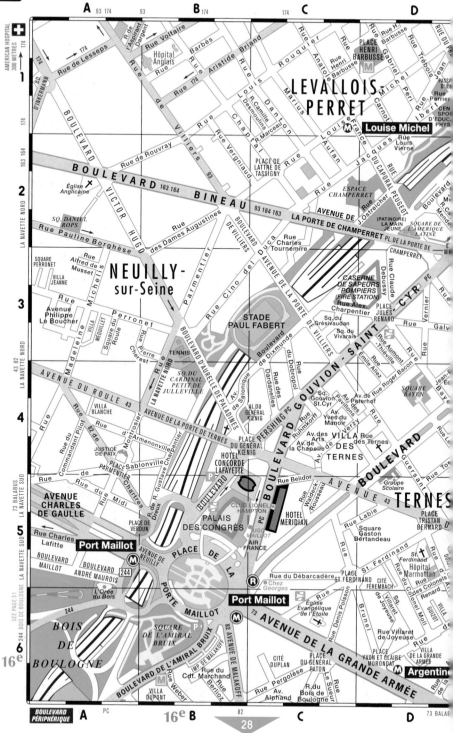

AMERICAN HOSPITAL
300 METRES

Bd. d'INNERMANN

R. de l'Aspirant Dargent

Rue Voltaire

Hôpital
Anglais
Rue

Barbès
Rue

Rue 174

Aristide Briand

Rue de Lesseps

174

Rue de Villiers

BOULEVARD

Louis R. Camille Desmoulins

R.Marceau

Chaptal

Rue Vergniaud

Marius

Louis Danton

Rue 174

Rue d'Anatole

Rouquier

Rue Henri

Rue Henri Barbusse

PLACE HENRI BARBUSSE

Rue Gabriel Péri

Rue H.
Barbusse

Rue Trébois

RUE DU
PEAN

Iber

Michel

Carnot

Perier

PASSA
D'IER

CEN
SPO
D'EDUC.
PHYS

Rue Perrier

LEVALLOIS-
PERRET

Jacques

Louise Michel

France

J. Auran

Rue

Louise Michel

Rue Louis Vierne

BOULEVARD 163 164 BINEAU

Église
Anglicaine

SQ. DANIEL
ROPS

Rue Pauline Borghèse

VICTOR HUGO

Rue de Rouvray

Rue des Dames Augustines

93

PLACE DE LATTRE DE TASSIGNY

Rue Cino del Duca

AVENUE DE LA PORTE DE CHAMPERRET 93 164 163

ESPACE CHAMPERRET

Rue J. Ostreicher

AVENUE DE

Rue Charles Tournemire

(PATINOIRE) LA MAIN JEUNE

SQUARE DE L'AMERIQUE LATINE

PL. DE LA PORTE DE CHAMPERRET

Boulevard

M

Mende

NEUILLY-
sur-Seine

SQUARE PERRONET

VILLA JEANNE

Rue Alfred de Musset

Michelis

Madeleine

AVENUE DU ROULE 43

Perronet

Square du Roule

Cherest

Pierre

Rue

Avenue Philippe Le Boucher

Rue

MEQUILLET

VILLA

Rue du Commandant Pilot

82 de

Montrosier

d'Armenonville

JUSTICE DE PAIX

PLACE Sablonville

de

PARMENTIER

Chartres

Rue de Dreux

Rue du Midi

BOULEVARD D'AURELLE DE PALADINES

BOULEVARD NORD

TENNIS

SQ. DU CARDINAL PETIT DE JULLEVILLE

Gustave Charpentier

Rue R.

AVENUE DE LA PORTE DE TERNES

PLACE DU GENERAL KŒNIG

HOTEL CONCORDE LAFAYETTE

BOULEVARD

DE VILLIERS

Boulevard du Dixmunde

STADE PAUL FABERT

Boulevard

du Dobropol

Rue des Dardanelles

AV. DU GENERAL KŒNIG

AV. de Salonique

PLACE DU GENERAL KŒNIG

Rue Charles Debussy

Rue Claude Debussy

CASERNE DE SAPEURS POMPIERS (FIRE STATION)

Rue Alex. Charpentier

Sq.du Grésivaudan

Sq. du Vivarais

Rue Aumont-Thiéville

Rue Emile Allez

Rue Roger Bacon

PLACE JULES RENARD

Rue

Vernier

Galv

Rue

SQUARE BAYEN

Jean-F

Baye

GOUVION-SAINT-CYR

PC

BOULEVARD

Sq. Gouvion St.Cyr

Av.des Pavillons

Av.de Peterhof

Av. Yves du Manoir

VILLA DES TERNES

Rue des Ternes

Guersant

BOULEVARD

Rue

Rue To

Verzy

Av. Ruhmkorff

Av.des Arts

Av.de la Chapelle

AV-Le

PERSHING PC

Rue Belidor

AVENUE

Groupe Scolaire

43

TERNES

PLACE TRISTAN BERNARD

D

CLUB LIONEL HAMPTON

Waldeck-Rousseau

HUGO MAILLOT

Rue Labie

Square Gaston Bertandeau

HOTEL MERIDIAN

St. Ferdinand

Hôpital Marmottan

AVENUE CHARLES DE GAULLE

Rue Charles Lafitte

BOULEVARD MAILLOT

BOULEVARD ANDRÉ MAUROIS

244

Port Maillot

AVENUE DE NEUILLY

PLACE DE VERDUN

PALAIS DES CONGRÈS

AIR FRANCE

Chez Georges

R

Port Maillot

Rue du Débarcadère

PLACE ST.FERDINAND

St.Ferdinand

CITÉ FEREMBACH

Rue des Colonels Renard

VILLA de JOYEUSE

GUIZOT

VILLA

SEE PAGE 51

BOIS DE BOULOGNE

244 BOIS DE BOULOGNE

LA NAVETTE SUD

L'Orée du Bois

BOIS
DE
BOULOGNE

244

SQUARE DE L'AMIRAL BRUIX

PLACE DE LA

PORTE MAILLOT

P

Port Maillot

73

Église Evangélique de l'Étoile

R.du Bois de Boulogne

Rue Denis Poisson

Brunel

Rue Villaret de Joyeuse

PLACE YVON ET CLAIRE MORONDAT

VILLA DE LA GRANDE ARMÉE

Argentine

16e

BOULEVARD PÉRIPHÉRIQUE

BOULEVARD DE L'AMIRAL MALAKOFF

IMP.DE MALAKOFF

Rue du Cdt. Marchand

Rue Weber

Rue Berlioz

VILLA DUPONT

AVENUE DE MALAKOFF

CITÉ DUPLAN

PLACE DU GENERAL PATON

Rue Pergolèse

Av. Alphand

R.du Bois de Boulogne

Rue de Sueur

AVENUE DE LA GRANDE ARMÉE

Rue de la

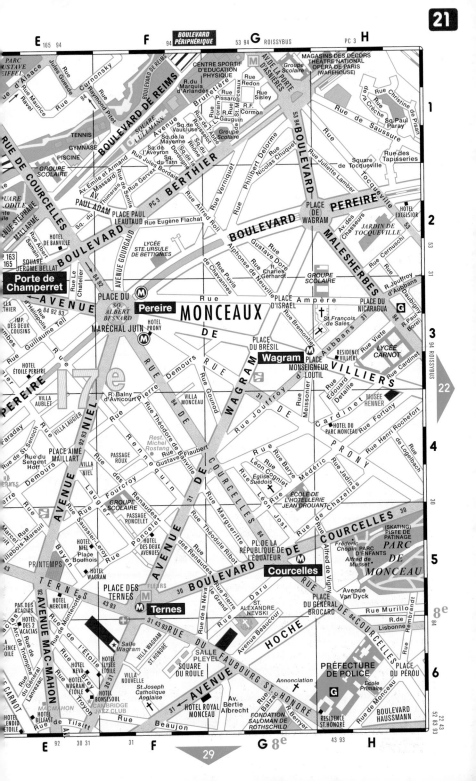

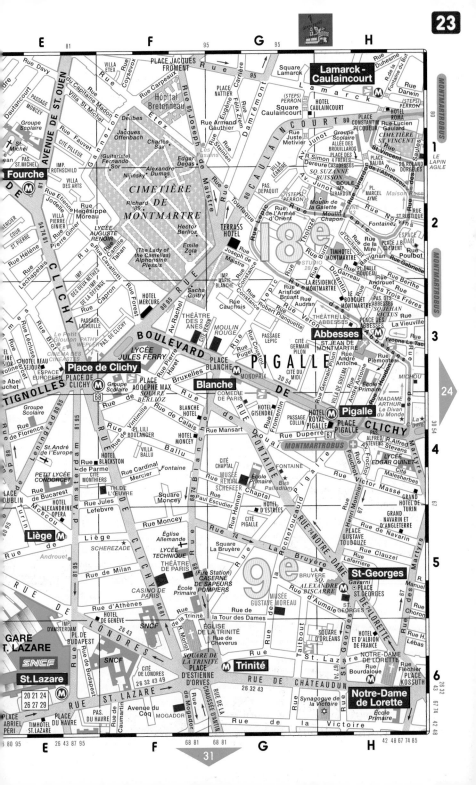

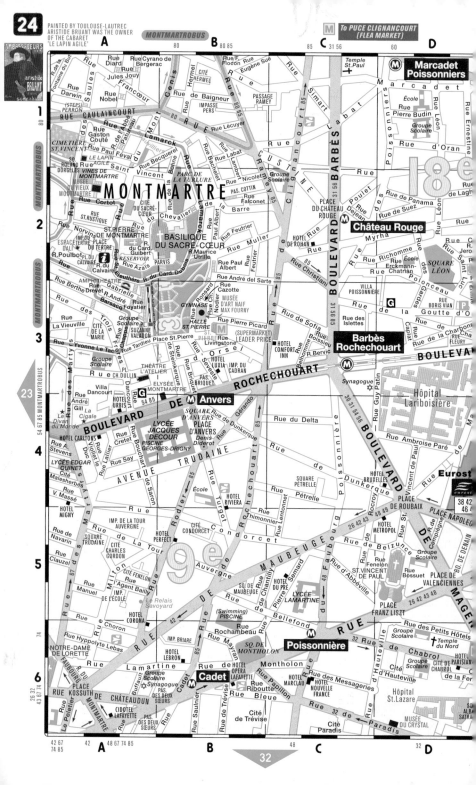

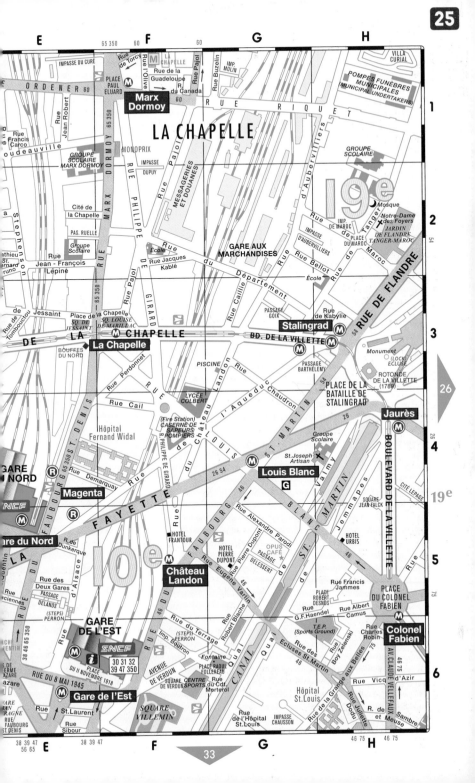

E 65 350 60 F 60 G H

IMPASSE DU CURÉ
R. de Torcy
CHAPELLE
Rue de l'Olive
Rue Pajol
IMP. BUZELIN
IMP. MOLIN
VILLA CURIAL

ORDENER 60
Rue Jean Robert
PLACE PAUL ELUARD
Rue de la Guadeloupe
R. du Canada
RUE RIQUET
POMPES FUNÈBRES MUNICIPALES MUNICIPAL UNDERTAKERS

Marx Dormoy M

Rue Francis Carco
oudeauville
MONOPRIX
LA CHAPELLE
GROUPE SCOLAIRE

1

GROUPE SCOLAIRE MARX DORMOY
IMPASSE DUPUY
MESSAGERIES ET DOUANES
d'Aubervilliers
19e
Mosquée

Cité de la Chapelle
PAS. RUELLE
Groupe Scolaire
Rue Jean-François Lépine
Rue Jacques Kablé
GARE AUX MARCHANDISES
Rue Bellot
IMP. DE MAROC
IMPASSE D'AUBERVILLIERS
PLACE DU MAROC
Notre-Dame des Foyers
JARDIN DE FLANDRE
TANGER-MAROC

2

Rue de Tombouctou
Jessaint
Place de la Chapelle
SQ. LOUISE DE MARILLAC
Rue Caillié
du Département
École
Rue de Maroc

DE LA CHAPELLE
M **La Chapelle**
BOUFFES DU NORD
PASSAGE GOIX
Rue de Kabylie
Stalingrad M
BD. DE LA VILLETTE M
RUE DE FLANDRE

3 54

Rue Perdonnet
PISCINE
Rue Landon
PASSAGE BARTHÉLEMY
Monument
(LOCK) ÉCLUSE
ROTONDE DE LA VILLETTE (1789)
26 →

Rue Cail
LYCÉE COLBERT
l'Aqueduc Chaudron
St. Martin
PLACE DE LA BATAILLE DE STALINGRAD

ST. DENIS
Hôpital Fernand Widal
(Fire Station) CASERNE DE SAPEURS POMPIERS
R. PHILIPPE DE GIRARD
du Château
Rue Louis
Jaurès M
BOULEVARD DE LA VILLETTE

4 26

GARE DU NORD R
Rue Demarquay
26 54
M
St. Joseph Artisan
Louis Blanc G
Groupe Scolaire
Valmy
Jemmapes
SQUARE JEAN-FALCK
CITÉ LEPAGE
19e

Magenta R
SNCF M
Gare du Nord
R. de Dunkerque
FAUBOURG
FAYETTE
10e
HOTEL FRANTOUR
Rue Alexandre Parodi
OPUS CAFÉ
BLANC
St. MARTIN
HOTEL URBIS
5 75

Rue des Deux Gares
PASSAGE DELANOS
(STEPS) PERRON
Château Landon M
HOTEL PIERRE DUPONT
Rue Eugène Varlin
Rue Pierre Dupont
PASSAGE DELESSERT
PLACE ROBERT DESNOS
Rue Francis Jammes
G.F.Haendel
Rue Albert Camus
PLACE DU COLONEL FABIEN

GARE DE L'EST
M i SNCF
30 31 32 39 47 350
Rue du Terrage
(STEPS) PERRON
IMP. Béruton
Robert Blache
T.E.P. (Sports Ground)
Rue des Écluses St-Martin
Boy Zelenski
Rue Charles Robin
Colonel Fabien M
AV. CLAUDE VELLEFAUX d'Azir
6 75

PLACE DU 11 NOVEMBRE 1918
AVENUE DE VERDUN
Fontaine
PLACE RAOUL FOLLEREAU
CANAL
Rue Vicq

Gare de l'Est M
RUE DU 8 MAI 1945
SQUARE CENTRE DE VERDUN SPORTS
Rue du Cdt. Mortérol
Hôpital St.Louis
Rue de la Grange aux Belles
Rue Juliette Dodu
R. de Sambre et Meuse

RUE FAUBOURG
St. Laurent
Rue Sibour
SQUARE VILLEMIN
Rue de l'Hôpital St.Louis
IMPASSE CHAUSSON

38 39 47 56 65
E
38 39 47
F
33 ↓
G
46 75
H
46 75

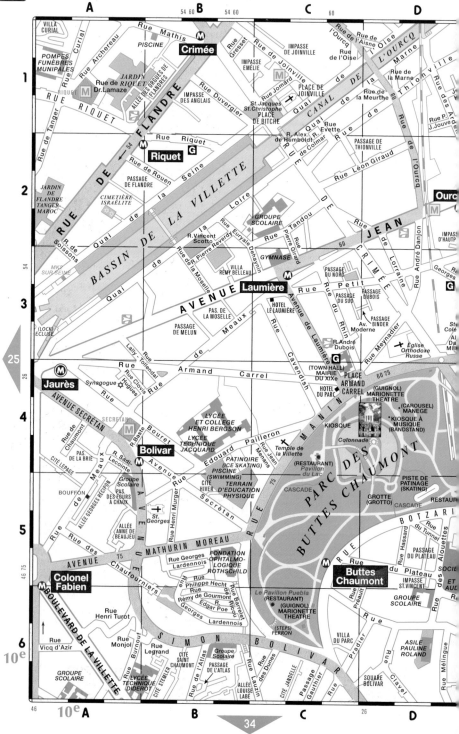

A 54 60 B 54 60 C 60 D

VILLA
CURIAL
Rue Mathis
POMPES
FUNÈBRES
MUNIPALES
PISCINE
Crimée
Rue Gresset
Rue de Joinville
IMPASSE
DE JOINVILLE
Rue de l'Ourcq
Rue de l'Aisne Oise
Rue de l'Ourcq

JARDIN
DE RIQUET
Dr.Lamaze
Rue Duverger
IMPASSE EMÉLIE
PLACE DE JOINVILLE
Rue de la Marne
Rue de la Meurthe

1

IMPASSE DES ANGLAIS
Rue Jomard
St.Jacques St.Christophe
PLACE DE BITCHE
R. Alex. de Humboldt
Quai
Rue Evette
Rue de Colmar

Riquet
Rue Riquet
G
Seine
R.Vincent Scotto
Rue Léon Giraud
PASSAGE DE THIONVILLE

PASSAGE DE FLANDRE
Rue de Rouen
CIMETIÈRE ISRAÉLITE
Loire
GROUPE SCOLAIRE
Rue Euryale Dehaynin
Rue Tandou
Rue Pierre Girard

2
JARDIN DE FLANDRE TANGER-MAROC
Quai
de
la
Rue de la Moselle
Pierre reverdy
GYMNASE
VILLA RÉMY BELLEAU

MKZ SUR SEINE
BASSIN DE LA VILLETTE
Rue de R.
Laumière
PASSAGE DU NORD
Rue Petit
PASSAGE DUBOIS

(LOCK) ECLUSE
AVENUE
PAS. DE LA MOSELLE
HOTEL LE LAUMIÈRE
Avenue de Laumière
Rue du Rhin
PASSAGE DU SUD
PASSAGE BINDER
Av. Moderne

3
PASSAGE DE MELUN
de
Meaux
R.André Dubois
Rue Meynadier
Église Orthodoxe Russe

Lally - Tolendal
Rue
Armand
Carrel
Cavendish
G
(TOWN HALL) MAIRIE DU XIXe
PLACE ARMAND CARREL

Jaurès
Rue Clovis Hugues
Synagogue
Rue
HOTEL DU PARC
(GUIGNOL) MARIONETTE THEATRE
(CAROUSEL) MANEGE

AVENUE SECRETAIN
SECRETAN
R.Baste Bouret
LYCEE ET COLLEGE HENRI BERGSON
Pailleron
Rue Jean Menans
KIOSQUE
KIOSQUE À MUSIQUE (BANDSTAND)

4
Rue de Chaumont
R.Sadi. Lecointe
Bolivar
LYCEE TECHNIQUE JACQUARD
Edouard
Temple de la Villette
Colonnade
PARC DES

PAS. DE LA BRIE
CITÉ LEPAGE
Groupe Scolaire
Avenue
PATINOIRE (ICE SKATING) PISCINE (SWIMMING)
(Restaurant) Pavillon du Lac
PISTE DE PATINAGE (SKATING)

BOUFFON
PAS. DES COURS A CHAUX
Secrétan
CITÉ HIVER
TERRAIN D'EDUCATION PHYSIQUE
CASCADE
GROTTE (GROTTO)
RESTAUR

5
ALLÉE GEORGES RECIPON
St. Georges
MATHURIN MOREAU
Rue Henri Murger
CASCADE
BUTTES CHAUMONT
BOTZARI
Rue du tunnel

ALLÉE ANNE DE BEAUJEU
AVENUE
Chaufourniers
FONDATION OPHTALMO-LOGIQUE ROTHSCHILD
RUE MANIN
PASSAGE DU PLATEAU

Colonel Fabien
Rue des
Rue Georges Lardennois
Rue Philippe Hecht
Buttes Chaumont
Rue du Plateau
IMPASSE ST.VINCENT
SOCIE ET AUD

6
Rue Henri Turot
Rue de Gourmont
R. Edgar Poe
R. Georges
Barellet
Le Pavillon Puebla (RESTAURANT)
(GUIGNOL) MARIONETTE THEATRE
GROUPE SCOLAIRE
VILLA DU PARC

Rue Monjol
Rue Burnouf
Rue Legrand
CITÉ SAINT CHAUMONT
Groupe Scolaire
PASSAGE DE L'ATLAS
(STEPS) PERRON
Rue Pradier
ASILE PAULINE ROLAND

10e
Rue Vicq d'Azir
SIMON
BOLIVAR
Rue de l'Atlas
ALLÉE LOUISE LABE
SQUARE BOLIVAR
Rue Clavel
Rue Mélingue

GROUPE SCOLAIRE
LYCEE TECHNIQUE DIDEROT
CITÉ STEMLER
CITÉ JANDELLE
Passage Gauthier

10e A 46 B 34 C 26 D

25 26

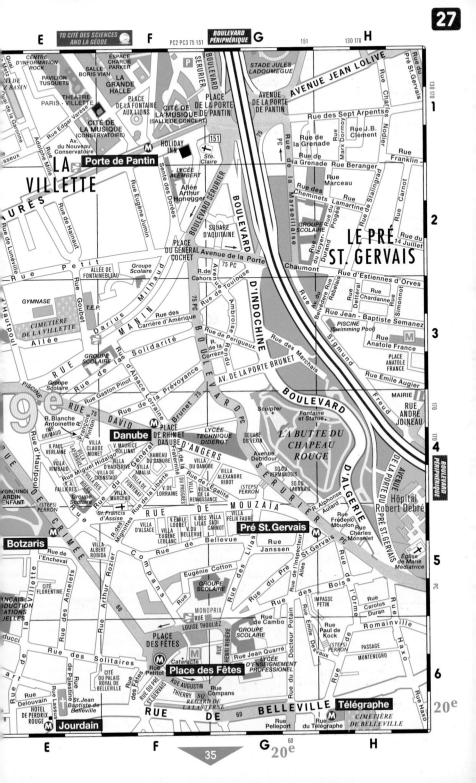

SEE PAGE 51
BOIS DE BOULOGNE
20

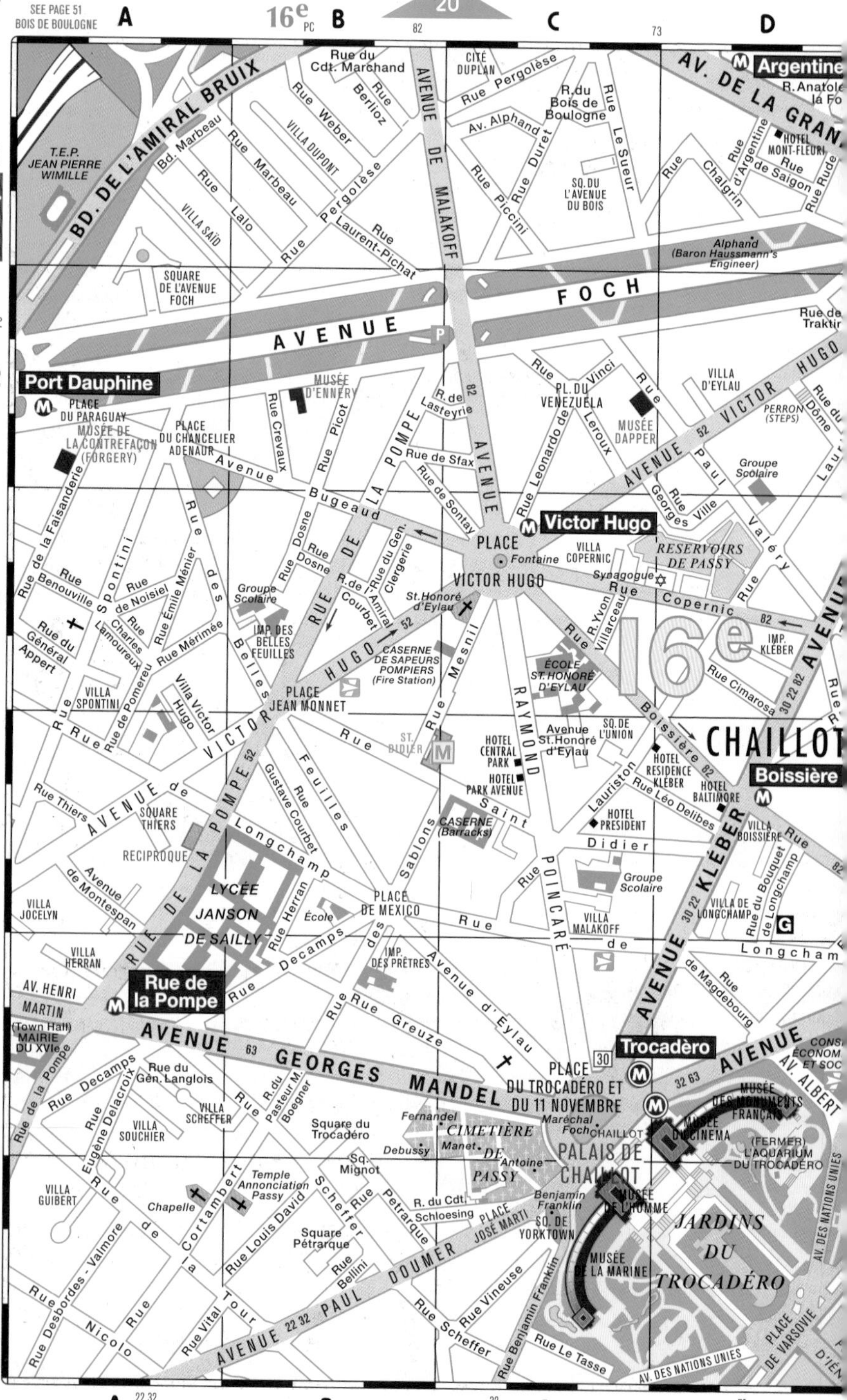

36

Map labels:

29

7e E 92 30 31 F 21 31 8e G 43 93 H

Hotel RELAIS
Hotel MAC-MAHON
LENDLO cine a
MAC-MAHON
AV. DE WAGRAM
St.Joseph Catholique Anglaise
Rue
HOCHE
Av. Bertie Albrecht
HÔTEL ROYAL MONCEAU
PRÉFECTURE DE POLICE
Rue de Monceau
R. de Courcelles
22 43 52 83 93

AV. CARNOT
AV. DE Tilsitt
AV. MAC-MAHON
AV. HOCHE
Beaujon
Rue Balzac
RUE DU FAUBOURG ST.-HONORÉ
Rue Berryer
FONDATION SALOMON DE ROTHSCHILD
PLACE GEORGES GUILLAUMIN
HÔTEL FRIEDLAND
83
Rue de Berri
BD. HAUSSMANN
52

Charles de Gaulle Étoile
Ⓜ
AVENUE DE FRIEDLAND
Chapelle du Corpus Christi
Le Garage
1

MÉE
ARC DE TRIOMPHE (1836)
Ⓜ AV. NAPOLÉON
22 52
Tombeau du 'Soldat Inconnu' (Unknown Soldier)
Rue Arsène
Rue Balzac
Rue Lord Byron
Rue Châteaubriand
Washington
CHAMBRE DE COMMERCE
Teillevent Lamennais
Berri
d'Arlo St. Philippe du Roule

PLACE CHARLES DE GAULLE
de
Presbourg
Rue Arène Danois
Église Danois
UGC GEORGE V
CITÉ ODIOT
IMPASSE FORTIN Frédéric Bastiat
ÉLYSÉES HÔTEL
52

KLÉBER
AVENUE
Pub Winston Churchill's
PUBLICIS ÉLYSÉES
LE BALZAC
UGC NORMANDIE
AVENUE DES CHAMPS-ÉLYSÉES
HÔTEL LE WARWICK
Rue de
HÔTEL CALIFORNIA
Rue Paul Baudry
École
ÉLYSÉES HÔTEL
DON CAMILO

Kléber
George V
Ⓜ
LIDO
73
GALERIE DES CHAMPS
ARCADES DU LIDO
GALERIE POINT SHOW
ÉLÉPHANT BLEU
GALERIE ÉLYSÉES LA BOÉTIE
2

AV. des Portugais
Rue Newton
Rue Euler
ARC DE TRIOMPHE
Rue Vernet
Galilée
LE FOUQUET'S
UGC BIARRITZ
GALERIE DU CLARIDGE
ERMITAGE
UGC
GAUMONT CHAMPS ÉLYSÉES
MONOPRIX
VIRGIN

JNESCO
RUE Quentin
PL. Jacquemin St-George's
RICHARD DE COUDENHOVE KALERGI
Rue Keppler
HÔTEL KEPPLER
Rue Bassano
Rue Magellan
Rue Quentin
PL HENRY DUNANT
Rue Christophe Colomb
Bauchart
Rue Lincoln
ÉLYSÉES LINCOLN
CHAMPS ÉLYSÉES
CABARET GAUMONT AMBASSADE
GAUMONT MARIGNAN
Rue du Colisée
GALERIE ÉLYSÉES
DISNEY STORE
26
32 73

AVENUE D'IÉNA
PLACE DE L'URUGUAY
Rue Auguste Vacquerie
Galilée
Rue Jean Giraudoux
Bassano
Rue Pierre Charron
NOVA PARK ÉLYSÉES
Bashir
Franklin D. Roosevelt
Ⓜ
Man Ray
Rue Robert Estienne
Groupe Scolaire
CHAMPS-ÉLYSÉES
3

y Washington & Lafayette
PLACE DES ÉTATS UNIS
Rue
de
Dumont d'Uville
PLACE DE CHAILLOT
HÔTEL MARRIOTT PRINCE
QUEEN ELIZABETH HOTEL
HÔTEL GEORGE V
CHÂTEAU FRONTENAC
HÔTEL CLARIDGE BELLMAN
RUE François
IMP. BOURDIN
Élysée Matignon
IMP. RUFIN
42 80
30

Aux Volontaires, Américains Morts pour La France
de l'Amiral d'Estaing
SQ. DE CHAILLOT
Rue Georges
DR. J.BERTILLON
IMP. DU
LES CALVADOS
AMERICAN CATHEDRAL
R.de la Renaissance
Rue du Boccador
Rue Clément Marot
CANADIAN EMBASSY
42 80

Lübeck
MUSÉE GUIMET
AVENUE D'IÉNA
PLACE ROCHAMBEAU
Rue de la MODE ET DU COSTUME
PALAIS GALLIERA MUSÉE DE LA MODE ET COSTUME
Rue Freycinet
St Pierre de Chaillot
PIERRE 1er DE SERBIE
PLACE PIERRE BRISSON
Orthodoxe Grecque
Rue Goethe
RUE DE LA TRÉMOILLE
Chez Edgard
Rue Édgard
Rue Marbeuf
Rue Chambiges
HÔTEL PLAZA ATHÉNÉE
1er
PLACE FRANÇOIS 1er
HÔTEL SAN REGIS
4

Rue de Galliera
Brignole
Rue Léonce Reynaud
CRAZY HORSE
AVENUE MONTAIGNE
Le Relais Plaza
COMÉDIE ET THÉÂTRE DES CHAMPS-ÉLYSÉES
Rue Jean Goujon
Église Arménienne
Bayard

PLACE George Washington
PRÉSIDENT
Ⓜ 63
WILSON
Alma Marceau
Ⓜ
Chez Francis
PL DE LA REINE ASTRID
HÔTEL ROYAL ALMA

Ⓜ D'IÉNA
Iéna
Ⓜ
MUSÉE D'ART MODERNE DE LA VILLE DE PARIS
PALAIS DE TOKYO
Rue de la Manutention
Rue G.Raston St.Paul
Rue G.Debrousse
Périer
R. des Frères
Liberté Flamme (New York)
SHRINE TO PRINCESS DIANA
PLACE DE L'ALMA
Ⓜ
Mickiewicz Monument (Bourdelle)
(STEPS) PERRON
COURS ALBERT 1er
PORT DE LA CONFÉRENCE
72
5

AVENUE DE NEW YORK
Rue Fresnel
Rue Foucauld
footbridge PASSERELLE DEBILLY
Pont de l'Alma
PONT DE L'ALMA
VOIE GEORGES POMPIDOU
BATEAUX MOUCHES

VOIE GEORGES POMPIDOU
SEINE
S
PORT DEBILLY
PORT DE LA BOURDONNAIS
42
PLACE DE LA RÉSISTANCE
Ⓡ
(SEWERS) LES ÉGOUTS DE PARIS
PORT DU GROS CAILLOU
QUAI D'ORSAY
(STEPS) PERRON
63
6

ATEAUX RISIENS
QUAI BRANLY
AV. DE LA BOURDONNAIS
CENTRE DE CONFÉRENCES ESPACE EIFFEL - BRANLY
Avenue Franco-Russe
AVENUE RAPP
AV. BOSQUET
CITÉ DE L'ALMA
Rue Cognacq-Jay
Rue du Col. Combes
RADIODIFFUSION TÉLÉVISION FRANÇAISE
Église Américaine
Rue
l'Université
VILLA BOSQUET
Passage LAMIRIEU
Malar
ST PIERRE DU GROS CAILLOU
Rue Henri Moissan
Av. Robert Schumann
Av. Sully-Prudhomme
Jean Nicot
Ⓜ
PASSAGE COMMUN
7e
69

E 42 F 7e G 80 92 H 69

37

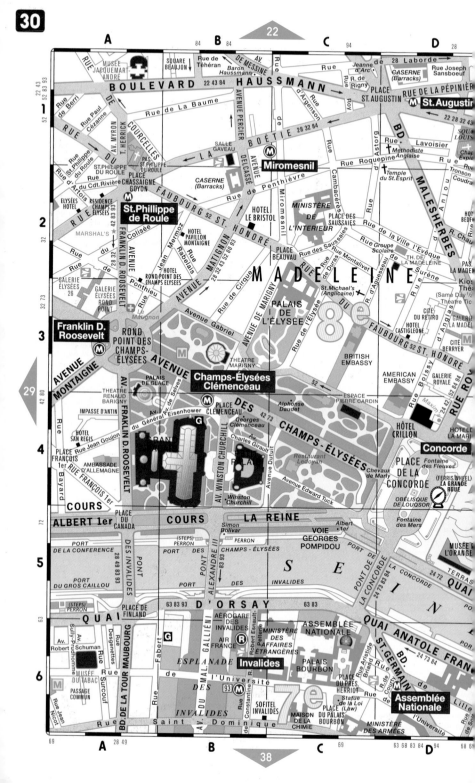

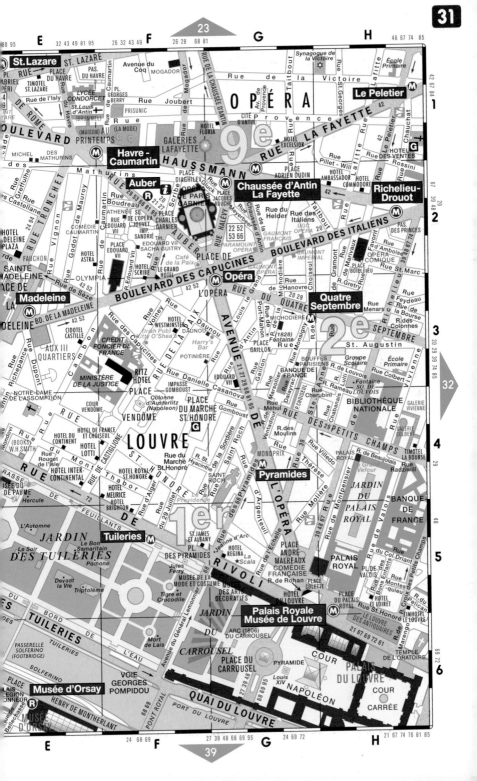

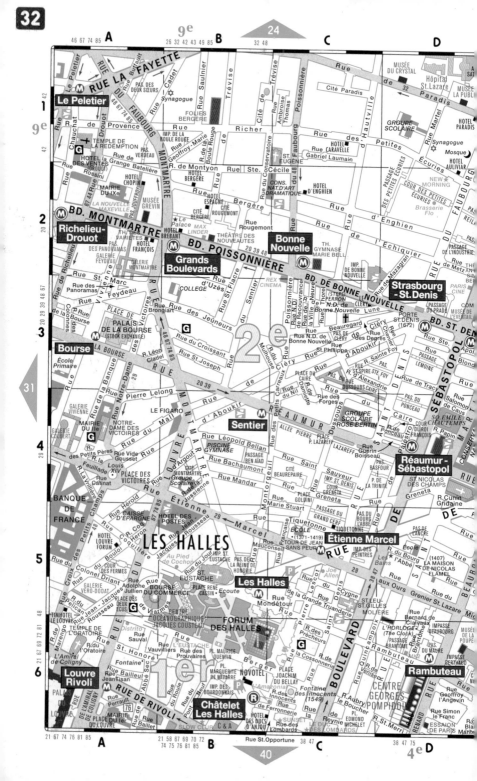

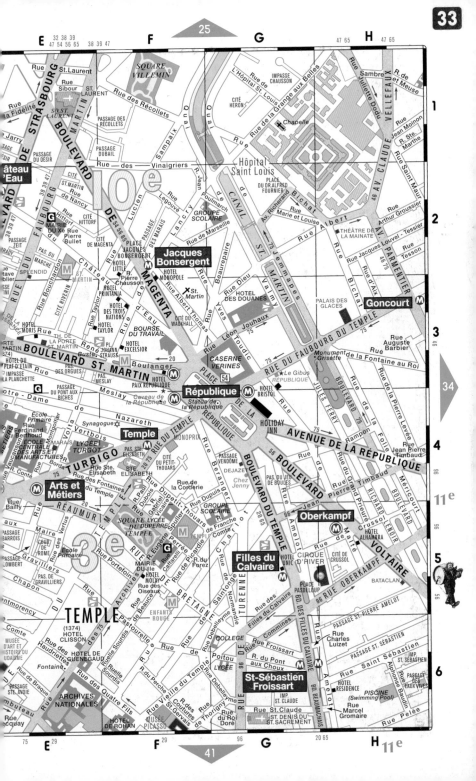

E 32 38 39   F   G   47 65 H 77 65
   47 54 65 65   38 39 47

Rue   St.Laurent
Rue
Sibour   ST.
                LAURENT
la Fidélité   Rue des Récollets
Rue
Jarry   PASSAGE DES
                RÉCOLLETS
SAGE
SIR   PASSAGE
                DUBAIL
âteau   PASSAGE
'Eau   DU DÉSIR   Rue - des - Vinaigriers

SQUARE
VILLEMIN

Rue l'Hôpital St.Louis
Rue   IMPASSE
                CHAUSSON
Rue de la Grange aux Belles
CITÉ
HÉRON
Chapelle

Hôpital
Saint Louis

PLACE
DU DR.ALFRED
FOURNIER

46 AV. CLAUDE VELLEFAUX

Sambre
et Meuse
R. de
R.
Juliette Dodu
R. Ste.
Jean Moinon
Marthe
Rue Saint Maur

1

CITÉ
ST. Histoir
ST. Rue
de Nancy

10e

BOULEVARD

DE STRASBOURG

CITÉ
DE MAGENTA

PLACE
JACQUES
BONSERGENT

HÔTEL
LITTLE
R. Pierre
Chausson

HÔTEL
PRINTANIA

HÔTEL
DES TROIS
NATIONS

HÔTEL
TAYLOR

HÔTEL
EXCELSIOR

Jacques
Bonsergent

HÔTEL
MONOPOLE

St.
Martin

CANAL

ST. MARTIN

QUAI

QUAI

GROUPE
SCOLAIRE

Rue de Marseille

Rue Pouimarch

Rue Richerand
Rue
Marie et Louise

Bichat

Albert

Rue

THÉÂTRE
DE
LA MAINATE

Rue Jacques Louvel - Tessier
46 75

Rue Tesson

Rue d'Aix

PALAIS DES
GLACES

Rue
Arthur Groussier

2

Goncourt

Rue
Auguste
Barbier

46

RUE DU FAUBOURG DU TEMPLE

de la Fontaine au Roi

3

34

HÔTEL
MORIS

BOULEVARD ST. MARTIN

BOURSE
DU TRAVAIL

CASERNE
VÉRINES

PLACE

République

Léon Jouhaux

Le Gibus

RÉPUBLIQUE

HÔTEL
BRISTOL

JULES FERRY

Rue de la Pierre Levée

Rampon

Rue
Jean Pierre
Timbaud

4

11e

96

Temple

TURGOT

Arts et
Métiers

RÉAUMUR

TEMPLE

3e

RUE DU TEMPLE

BOULEVARD DU TEMPLE

AVENUE DE LA RÉPUBLIQUE

HOLIDAY
INN

Oberkampf

Filles du
Calvaire

St-Sébastien
Froissart

ARCHIVES
NATIONALES

MUSÉE
PICASSO

VOLTAIRE

BATACLAN

CIRQUE
D'HIVER

PISCINE
(Swimming Pool)

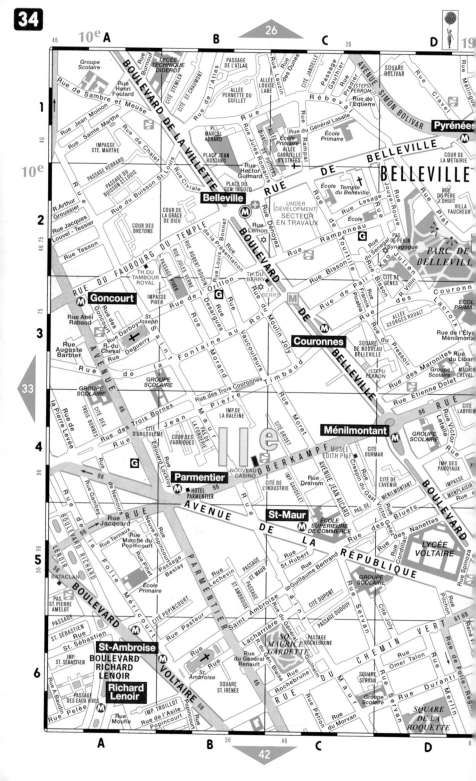

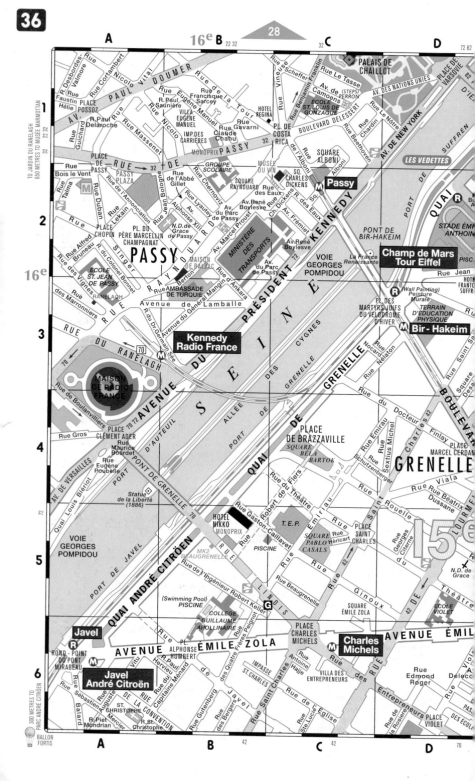

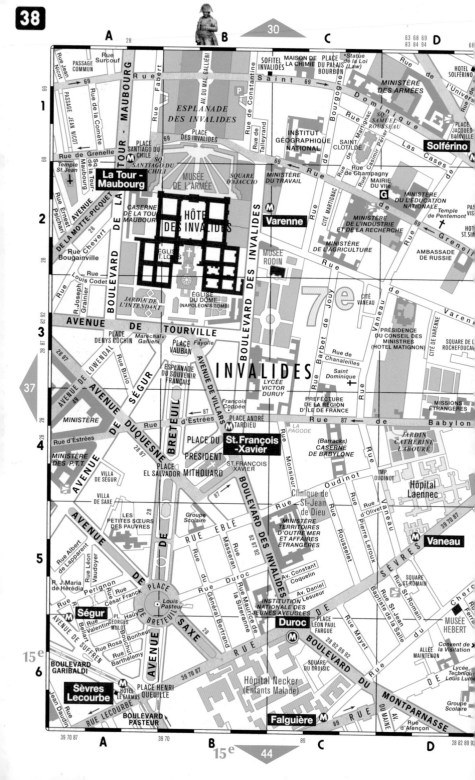

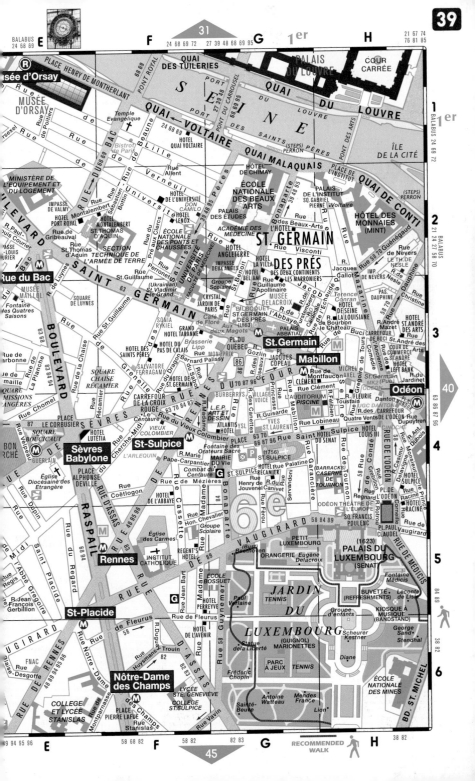

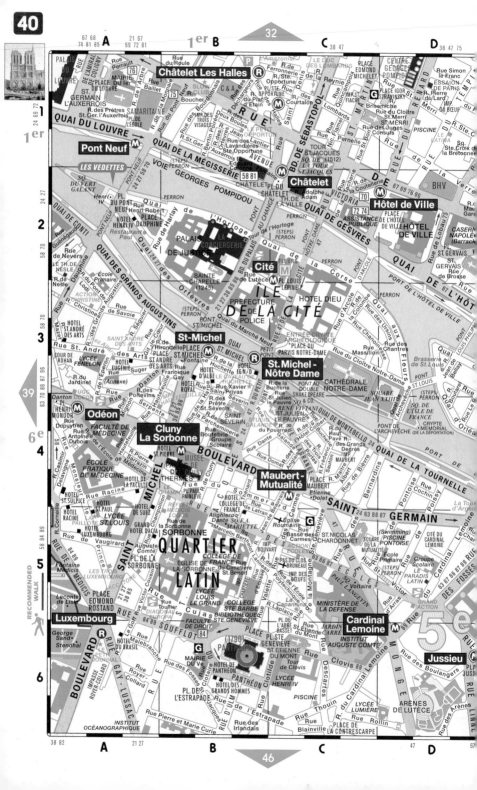

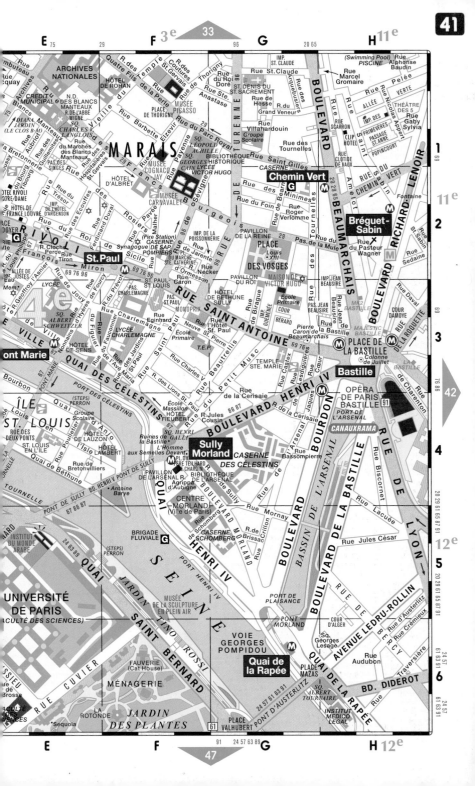

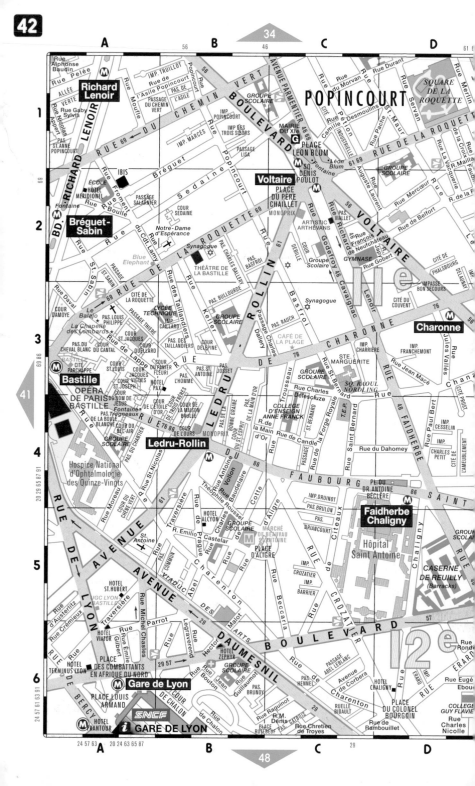

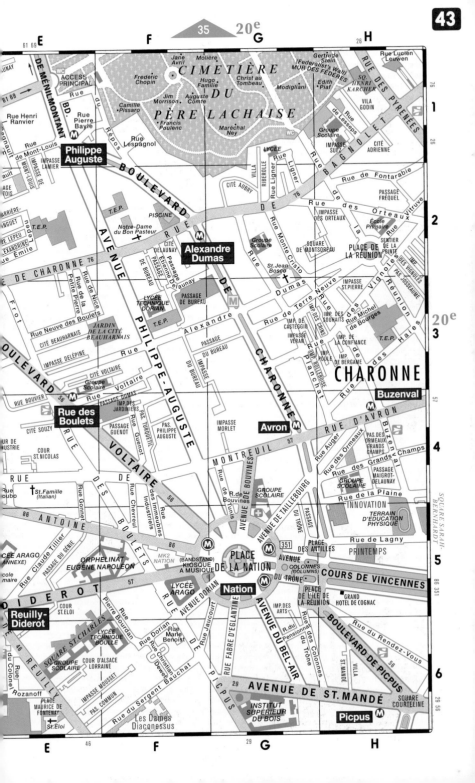

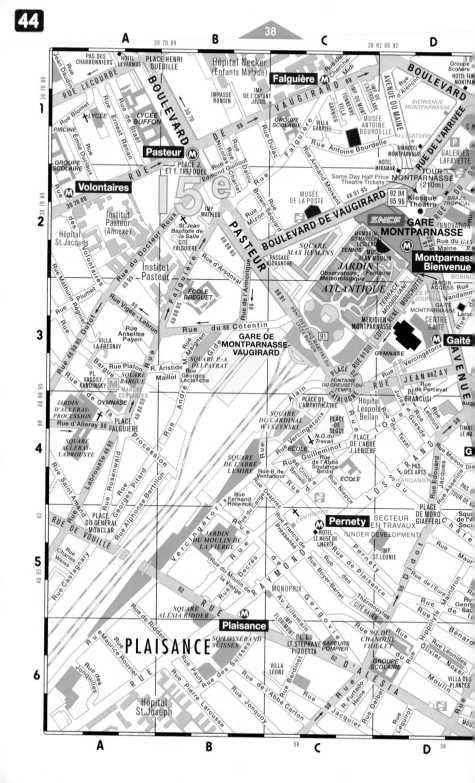

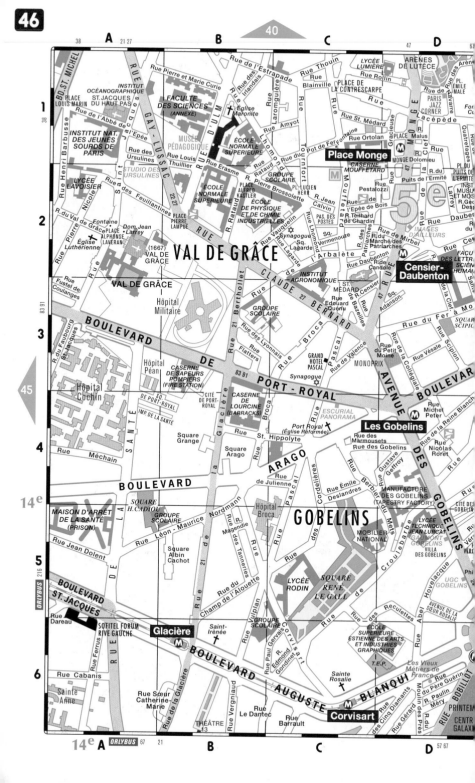

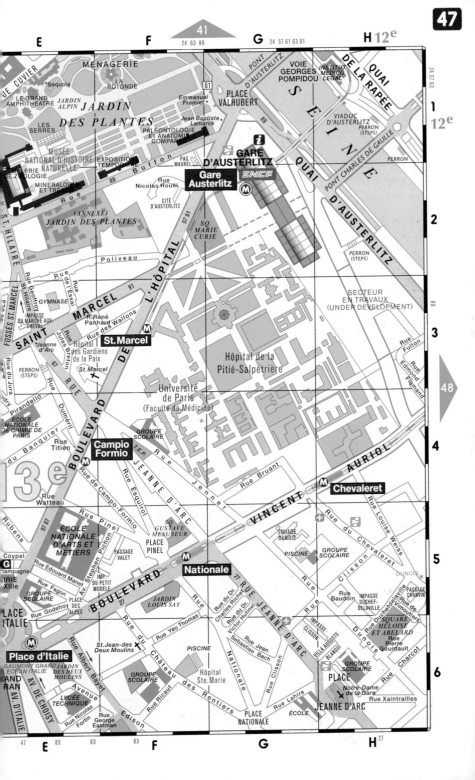

MENAGERIE

RUE CUVIER · Sequoia

LE GRAND AMPHITHEATRE

JARDIN ALPIN

LA ROTONDE

JARDIN

DES PLANTES

LES SERRES

MUSÉE NATIONAL D'HISTOIRE NATURELLE

GALERIE DE ZOOLOGIE

MINERALOGIE ET TREMORS

PALEONTOLOGIE ET ANATOMIE COMPARÉE

EXPOSITIONS TEMPORAIRE

Rue Buffon

Rue Nicolas Houël

CITÉ D'AUSTERLITZ

(ANNEXE) JARDIN DES PLANTES

Emmanuel Fremiet

Jean Baptiste Lamarck

PAS. MAUREL

PLACE VALHUBERT

GARE D'AUSTERLITZ

Gare Austerlitz

SNCF

VOIE GEORGES POMPIDOU

PONT D'AUSTERLITZ

INSTITUT MEDICO LEGAL

QUAI DE LA RAPÉE

SEINE

VIADUC D'AUSTERLITZ PERRON (STEPS)

PONT CHARLES DE GAULLE

PERRON

12e

QUAI D'AUSTERLITZ

1

RUE ST-HILAIRE

FOSSES ST-HILAIRE

Rue Geoffroy St-Hilaire

Poliveau

SQ. MARIE CURIE

SECTEUR EN TRAVAUX (UNDER DEVELOPMENT)

PERRON (STEPS)

2

GYMNASE

IMPASSE DU MARCHE AUX CHEVAL

RUE

BOULEVARD

SAINT

MARCEL

DE

L'HÔPITAL

R. René Panhard

Rue des Wallons

Jules Breton

Hôpital des Gardiens de la Paix

'Jeanne d'Arc'

St.Marcel

St.Marcel

Hôpital de la Pitié-Salpêtrière

Rue Fulton

Rue Edmond Flamand

3

Rue du Jura

PERRON (STEPS)

Pirandello

ECOLE NATIONALE DE CHIMIE DE PARIS

Rue Duméril

Rue du Banquier

Rue Titien

Campio Formio

Université de Paris (Faculté de Médicine)

GROUPE SCOLAIRE

T.E.P.

Rue Jenner

Rue Bruant

BOULEVARD

RUE JEANNE D'ARC

Rue de Campo-Formio

Rue Esquirol

RUE VINCENT

AURIOL

Chevaleret

48

4

13e

Rue Watteau

Rue Pinel

ECOLE NATIONALE D'ARTS ET MÉTIERS

Av. Stephen Pichon

PASSAGE VALET

PLACE PINEL

SQ GUSTAVE MESUREUR

SQUARE DUNOIS

PISCINE

GROUPE SCOLAIRE

Rue du Chevaleret

Rue Louise Weiss

Rue Clisson

5

Rubens

Coypel

Champagne

G

XIIIe

GROUPE SCOLAIRE

Rue Fagon

Rue Edouard Manet

PLACE DES ALPES

Rue Godefroy

IMP. DU PETIT MODÈLE

Nationale

BOULEVARD

JARDIN LOUIS SAY

Rue du Château des Rentiers

Rue Yéo Thomas

Rue du Dr. Charles Richet

Rue du Dr. Victor Hutinel

Rue Jean Sebastien Bach

Rue Clisson

IMPASSE VILLA AUGUSTE BLANQUI

Rue Baudoin

IMPASSE DUCHEF-DELAVILLE

Rue Duchefdelaville

Rue de Vimoutiers

PASSAGE CHANVIN

DUNOIS

SQUARE HÉLOISE ET ABELARD

Rue Pierre Gourdault

Rue Charcot

6

PLACE D'ITALIE

Place d'Italie

GAUMONT GRAND ECRAN ITALIE

AND RAN

AV. DE CHOISY

AVENUE D'ITALIE

St.Jean-des-Deux Moulins

JARDIN DES DEUX MOULINS

GROUPE SCOLAIRE

LYCÉE TECHNIQUE

Rue Nicolas Fortin

Rue George Eastman

Avenue Edison

Rue Ricaut

Rue Albert Bayet

PISCINE

Hôpital Ste.Marie

PLACE NATIONALE

Rue des Rentiers

ÉCOLE

Rue Lahire

RUE JEANNE D'ARC

Dunois

GROUPE SCOLAIRE

PLACE JEANNE D'ARC

Notre-Dame de la Gare

Rue Xaintrailles

Rue Charcot

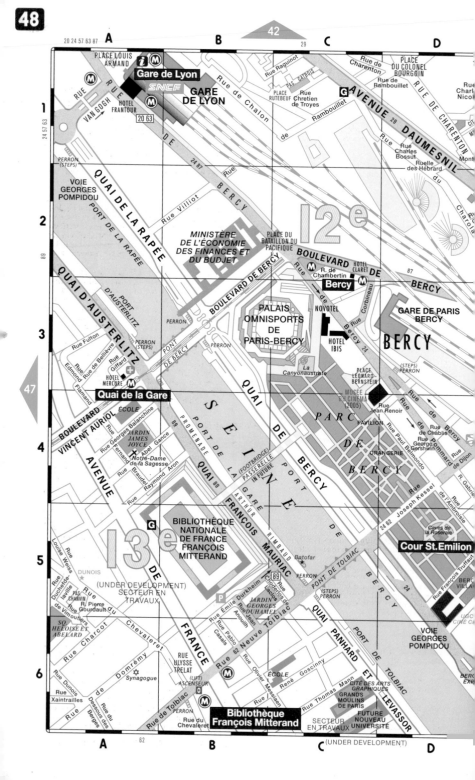

PARKS AND GARDENS

PARC DE BELLEVILLE   D2 34

Stand at the top of this terraced park near the rue des Envierges, and if you have seen the short, award winning film 'The Red Balloon', you will be able to recognise some of the buildings. If you fancy a baguette from the nearby café, you can have your picnic on one of the terraces. This is one of the highest parts of Paris, so it is a good viewpoint.

PARC DES BUTTES-CHAUMONT   C4 26

 Created in 1867, this is my favourite park. Once a bare hill (chaumont), until it was transformed by Adolphe Alphand (Haussmann's engineer) from a wasteland of disused quarries into a very beautiful picturesque park. There is a grotto, a lake, and in the centre a rocky island, which can be approached by a high suspension bridge. On the crest is a temple, from which there is an extensive view over Montmartre. Undulating and steep, with pleasant leafy avenues and some excellent restaurants (one overlooking the lake), the park is well worth a visit on a weekday.

JARDIN DU LUXEMBOURG   H5 39

These attractive gardens have, for many years, been a favoured place for students and families for that Sunday afternoon stroll. Everywhere you see statues, even a miniature 'Statue of Liberty' (G6). The gardens are a mixture of styles: there are English rows of chestnut trees, and French style flower beds, but unfortunately not a great deal of grass. There is a popular marionette theatre and several tennis courts. The 17th century Fontaine Médicis is a tranquil place to rest and watch the goldfish in the long pool. The palace commissioned by Queen Marie de Médicis in 1615, was a royal residence until the Revolution, when Camille Desmoulins and others were confined in it. Today, it houses the Senate of the Upper Assembly, one of the two Parliamentary chambers.

JARDIN DES TUILERIES   E5 31

The Tuileries Gardens were designed in the 17th century by the great Le Nôtre, the man responsible for the gardens at Versailles. Standing at the Louvre end of the gardens is the Arc du Carrousel. Built in 1806 and dedicated to Napoleon's armies, it is a lot smaller than the Arc de Triomphe, and much more colourful, finding it's inspiration from the Severus arch in Rome. It is topped by a quadriga (a four horse chariot): the horses are copies of the originals plundered from St. Mark's in Venice, and then returned as war reparation after Waterloo in 1815. From the Arc the views and perspectives are superb; Le Nôtre's historical axis now extends through the Arc de Triomphe onwards to the new Arche de La Défense. Today the gardens are full of sculptures in bronze and stone of every style and description, including many works by Aristide Maillol. On each side of the gardens are raised terraces for people to walk along, once very fashionable promenades.

PARC DE MONCEAU   A5 22

A strange beguiling place, laid out in the 18th century and very picturesque. Scattered between the trees are many interesting objects: a pagoda, pyramid, statues, ruins, and a Corinthian colonnade around a basin - like a Roman pool. There is also a Renaissance arc - a part of the old Hôtel de Ville that was set on fire during the Commune riots.

PARC MONTSOURIS not on the map see G6 45

Situated in the 14th arrondissement and reached by Line B of the RER (Métro). Cité Universitaire is the station to get off at. This is a very pleasant English style park with a lake, cascade, sloping lawns and a marvellous variety of trees. On the top of the hill on the southern side of the park is a replica of the Bardo, the Palace of the Bey of Tunisia, which was part of the exhibition of 1867.

SPORTS

TENNIS There are over 60 public courts in central Paris. Most are near the péripherique road, an exception being the courts in the Luxembourg gardens. The Roland Garros Stadium (see the map on Page 51) at the southern end of the Bois de Boulogne is the place for spectators. The French Open Championships are held here during the last week of May and first week in June.

FOOTBALL and RUGBY Also on the fringe of the Bois you will find the Parc des Princes (see Page 51). This is the ground for Paris St. Germain football club and the rugby team Racing Paris. International matches are played on this ground.

Off the map area on the north side at St. Denis is the modern Stade de France built for large events like the World Cup Final. Approached by Metro line 13 (Station Porte de Paris), or by RER line D or B (see map on Pages 2-3).

ICE SKATING - ROLLER SKATING La Main Jaune (D2 20) is a roller disco situated at the Porte de Champerret. For ice skating there is a rink near the Parc des Buttes-Chaumont (B4 26). Métro Bolivar

SWIMMING Each arrondissement has a public swimming pool and most are on the maps. The Piscine Pontoise (D5 40) is part of a sports complex, and is the swimming pool of the Latin Quarter.

Aquaboulevard is a massive aquatic and fitness complex - the largest in Europe. Here you will find giant water slides, rapide and a wave pool etc. Take the Métro to Balard the terminus of line 8 and walk down the avenue de la Porte de Sèvres. Worth a visit just to look!

HORSE RACING Paris has two racecourses; both are in the Bois de Boulogne. On the 3rd Sunday in June the French Steeplechase Grand Prix is held at Auteuil. Longchamp, however, is the most famous course in Paris - and justifiably so. On the first Sunday in October the Prix de l'Arc de Triomphe is held there. This event attracts winning horses and people from all parts of the globe. It is a World Championship,

PRIX DE L'ARC DE TRIOMPHE
Longchamp
DIMANCHE 1ᵉ OCTOBRE

final and Europe's richest race, dating back to 1920. On a fine Sunday in October I went to Longchamp with my wife. I had not been to a racecourse since my father took me to Newmarket to see the 1000 Guineas in 1949. That day I won backing an Australian jockey riding Musidora. Forty years on we won on every race - a memorable day. If you have never been before go early and head for Porte d'Auteuil (Métro). Outside the station waiting is a free coach shuttle (Navette Gratuite) which will take you to the main entrance. Everything you need is supplied free: programmes and English racing papers. You are unlikely to get a seat, so take a rug to sit on. Entrance to the terraces is about 4-8 euros, and you can use the grandstand facilities.

Betting At the back of the stands there are windows where you place your bets. They start at 2 euros. To bet 10 euros, go to the window which includes that denomination. To place a bet: Choose a horse. Give the horse's number on the programme
say GAGNANT - to win
or PLACE   - for a place (1st - 2nd - 3rd)

Once a dense wild wood, the Bois is part of the ancient Forest of Rouvray. When Napoleon was facing defeat, many trees were cut down and the wood was used to provide palisades as barriers against the approaching armies. After Waterloo, the forest was a camp for British and Prussian soldiers. It became a devastated piece of land, an extensive copse, until Baron Haussmann and his engineer, Adolphe Alphand, and gardeners set to work to create a park similar to London's Hyde Park. Trees were planted, cascades designed and two large lakes were laid out - the Lac Inférieur and Lac Supérieur. These were made using water from the artesian well at Passy. At the Carrefour de Longchamp, a 20 foot high rocky cascade (now covered with shrubs and ivy) was constructed, with an arc of rocks behind it rising to 40 feet. The Lac Inférieur has two islands and on one there is a chalet and restaurant, which can only be approached by a ferry from the east side. Further up the bank, rowing boats can be hired. Perhaps the best way to orientate yourself in this large park (2100 acres) is to hire a bike. These are available from April to October. The place to hire them is near the Jardin d'Acclimatation (see map).

PRÉ CATELAN Enclosed within the Bois is a lovely park, which also possesses one of the most romantic restaurants in Paris. Catelan is the name of a provençal poet who was murdered in the Bois and the Croix Catelan is the spot where his murderers were burnt. Very picturesque, the park claims to have a tree, a copper beech, which has a span wider than any other in the Paris area.

The Jardin Shakespeare is also enfolded in the Catelan park: a small, beautiful garden, it displays many trees, flowers and a small waterfall associated with the Bard's plays: The Tempest, As You Like It, Macbeth, Hamlet and A Midsummer's Night Dream. There is also an open air theatre performing Shakespeare, Molière etc. from May to September. Take bus number 244 from Porte Maillot and get off at Bagatelle: the bus route goes along the Allée de Longchamp. *Guided Tours 11.00 - 11.30, 15.00 - 15.30, and 16.00 - 17.30* *Charge*

PARC DE BAGATELLE If you want to escape from the noise and action of the city - perhaps a peaceful walk or a place to relax - then this exquisite park should be at the top of your list. There are waves of daffodils from March onwards, roses all through summer in the superb rose garden, an iris garden, and from June until October flowering clematis. By the black swan lake you can see magellan geese and peacocks. There are grottos, rock gardens, and in the autumn the trees are magnificent. Visiting is perfect at almost any time because the park has been so thoroughly co-ordinated and planned over the years. This is a Parisian Shangri-La.

Two of the highlights of the year in Bagatelle are the International New Rose competition, which is held in the gardens in June, and the Chopin Festival, which takes place in the Orangerie between about June 20th and July 14th. It is a particularly romantic setting for the piano recitals.

Built in just over sixty days as a wager, the house called Bagatelle was spared during the Revolution. It became the property of Sir Richard Wallace, famous for the Wallace art collection in London, and for donating over 100 drinking fountains to the city of Paris (which now owns Bagatelle). The gardens are reached by bus 244 from Porte Maillot (Métro). *Daily from 08.00* *Charge*

JARDIN D'ACCLIMATATION Situated in the NW corner of the Bois, the Jardin is an ideal place to bring children. Take the Métro to Porte Maillot station (A5 20), then you can ride the little train to the gardens. This is in service on school holidays, Wednesday, Saturday and Sunday, 13.30-18.00. On other days it is easier to go to Les Sablons station and walk 150 metres south. Some of the attractions are: a hall of mirrors, mini-moto cross, fairground, bowling, a small zoo (monkeys, bears etc) and a Norman farm with a self service restaurant where the animals (large ducks and sheep) wander around your table. *Daily 10.00 - 18.00 Charge*

Musée des Arts et Traditions Populaires This is in the confines of the Jardin and features French folk arts and crafts - the ethnological heritage of pre-industrial France. *Daily 09.45 - 17.15 Closed on Tuesday* *Charge*

MUSÉE MARMOTTAN Although today it is not really considered to be in the Bois, being on the eastern edge and detached by the péripherique road, the museum is sufficiently close to be included in this section. It faces the pleasant lawns of the English style Jardin du Ranelagh, and has one of France's most famous collections of Empire style furniture, and ranks only behind the Musee d'Orsay for impressionist art. There are many pictures by Claude Monet including the painting that baptised the movement, 'Impression, Sunrise' (1872). Take the Métro or RER train to La Muette and walk 200 metres west towards the Jardin du Ranelagh. Bus No.32 takes you close by. *Daily 10.00 - 17.30 Closed Monday* *Charge*

LES SERRES D'AUTEUIL Close by Porte d'Auteuil station at the SE tip of the Bois you will find the Municipal Floral Gardens: these are the gardens and greenhouses that supply Paris with its trees, plants and flowers. As you go in the main entrance at the end of a lawn there is an imposing palmarium, with tropical trees and plants. Throughout the winter, orchids are blooming in the greenhouses, and when spring comes the azaleas and begonias make the gardens a horticultural wonderland. *Daily 10.00 - 17.00 Autumn and Winter Spring and Summer 10.00 - 18.00* *Charge*

THE RACECOURSES I have already mentioned these on Page 49. Longchamp is the best. The Prix de l'Arc de Triomphe is a race in which colts and fillies, three years old and over, compete against each other. As most of them are champions, it makes the race the ultimate climax of the flat racing season. In a very attractive setting, this racecourse was inaugurated in 1857 by Napoleon III. Perhaps the most famous landmark of the course is the Moulin (windmill) which was once part of the Abbaye de Longchamp, founded in 1256. In the Tribune du Conseil (grandstand) you will find the Restaurant Panoramique where you can enjoy a splendid meal and at the same time have a superb view of the racing. The restaurant is very expensive on the day of the Arc, but on other days it can be quite reasonable. Going through the main entrance, you cannot miss the statue of Gladiateur, the first French horse to win the Epsom Derby in 1865.

Auteuil is the steeplechasing course. It is modern and you get a good view of the horses as they fly over the hedges and ditches.

It should be said that during the daytime the Bois is a very pleasant place, but as night proceeds the park is unfortunately descended upon by some less than desirable characters, so it is best to keep away!

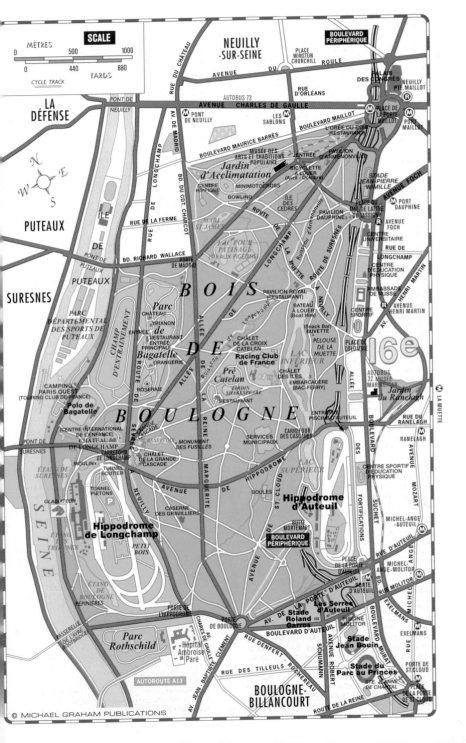

© MICHAEL GRAHAM PUBLICATIONS

BOIS DE VINCENNES

Philippe Auguste originally enclosed the Bois in 1183 to hold animals given to him by the King of England for hunting. It was not formerly laid out until 1860-67 on the orders of Napoleon III. Adolphe Alphand planned the lakes: Lac Daumesnil on the west side is the largest and contains two islands connected to each other and approached by a bridge from the south bank. Near the bridge is the Buddhist temple of Paris, which contains a massive effigy of Buddha. Further up the bank, rowing boats and bikes can be hired. In the NW corner of the Bois encompassed by a road is the Lac des Minimes; on the north bank is a restaurant - rowing boats can be hired here too.

LE CHÂTEAU DE VINCENNES
The best approach is from the Métro terminus of the same name. The château was the principal residence of the French kings until 1668 and the 53 metre high Donjon (keep) is the only remaining part of the fortress, built in 1328-50 by Philippe de Valois. Facing the Donjon is the Chapelle Royale constructed in the Gothic style and modelled on the Sainte Chapelle. The facade has an unusual rose window with a gable containing some fine tracery.

LE PARC FLORAL DE PARIS
An enchanting wood and floral garden created in 1969 and situated in the NE corner of the Bois. It has a small lake, fountains, plants and bushes. Among the other attractions are mini-golf, quadricycles, an adventure playground, table tennis and a mini train. *Daily 09.30 Closes May-Aug 20.00, Suns 21.00, Nov-Feb 17.00, March, September, October 18.00 Charge*

MUSÉE DES ARTS AFRICAINS ET OCÉANIENS
293 Av. Daumesnil, 75012. Métro Porte Dorée. The museum features arts and crafts from Africa and Oceania - weapons, pottery, masks - and a very interesting aquarium. · *10.00-12.00, 13.30-17.20. Sats, Suns 12.30-18.00, Closed Tuesday Charge*

HIPPODROME DE VINCENNES
This is not to compared with the courses in the Bois de Boulogne, as this track is for trotting races - horses in harness. The crowd is totally different too. Nevertheless this is the most popular racecourse in Paris for the punters. The best approach to the course is by RER (Métro) line number A2 to Joinville-le-Pont. Racing is held in the daytime and in the evening under floodlight. The Prix d'Amérique is the big race in trotting. This takes place at the end of January.

PARC ZOOLOGIQUE DE PARIS
53 Av. de St. Maurice 75012. A cleverly designed zoo inaugurated in 1934, and one of the most interesting I have ever been to; where possible the animals are in a natural environment or an assimilated one. The zoo was among the first to enclose animals with moats and walls. More than 1000 animals live here including: bears, tigers, giraffes, elephants, 110 species of mammals, together with over 140 species of birds, and rare animals such as panda, and okapi. As you approach the park you cannot fail to notice the Grand Rocher - a large man made rock that rises to a height of over 70 metres.

This is inhabited by sheep and goats; inside there is a lift and stairs that take you up to platforms from which there is a panoramic view over the park and surrounding area. Spring is a very good time to see the young ones - exuberant little monkeys trying to escape from their mothers' watchful eyes, baby elephants and hippos. Although audiovisual presentations are in French, they are easy to follow. They show the evolutionary process, the animals' ancestors, and how they have evolved over the years.

Feeding Times Pelicans - 14.15 Penguins - 14.30
Cats - 14.45 Sealions - 16.30
Métro Porte Dorée, bus numbers 46, 86, 325, PC *Daily Winter 09.00 to dusk. Charge Summer 09.00 - 18.00, Suns and Hols 09.00 -19.00*

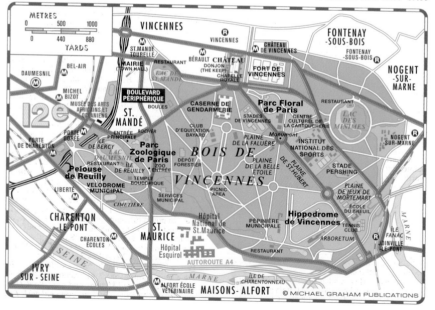

VERSAILLES

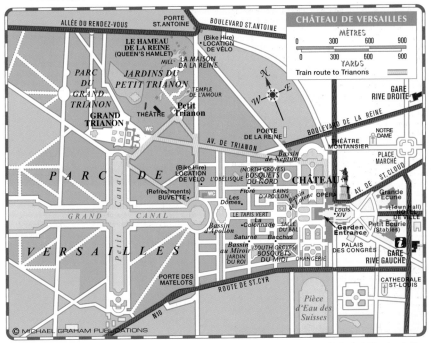

CHÂTEAU DE VERSAILLES

MÉTRES
0   300   600   900

YARDS
0   300   600   900

Train route to Trianons

ALLÉE DU RENDEZ-VOUS — PORTE ST.ANTOINE — BOULEVARD ST.ANTOINE

LE HAMEAU DE LA REINE (QUEEN'S HAMLET)
(Bike Hire) • LOCATION DE VÉLO
MILL
LA MAISON DA LA REINE

PARC DU GRAND TRIANON
JARDINS DU PETIT TRIANON
TEMPLE DE L'AMOUR

GARE RIVE DROITE

GRAND TRIANON
THÉÂTRE
Petit Trianon
WC
PORTE DE LA REINE
BOULEVARD DE LA REINE
THÉÂTRE MONTANSIER
NOTRE DAME
PLACE MARCHÉ

AV. DE TRIANON
Bassin de Neptune

P A R C   D E
(Bike Hire) LOCATION DE VÉLO
L'OBÉLISQUE
(NORTH GROVES) BOSQUETS DU NORD
CHÂTEAU
AV. DE ST.CLOUD

Grand Canal
Petit Canal
(Refreshments) BUVETTE •
WC
Flore Les Dômes
BAINS D'APOLLON
Bassin de Latone
OPÉRA
Grande Ecurie
(Town Hall) HOTEL DE VILLE
Louis XIV
Petit Ecurie (Stables)

G R A N D   C A N A L
LE TAPIS VERT
La Colonnade
SALLE DU BAL
Garden Entrance

Saturne Bacchus
PALAIS DES CONGRÈS
GARE RIVE GAUCHE

V E R S A I L L E S
Bassin d'Apollon
Bassin au Miroir
(SOUTH GROVES) BOSQUETS DU MIDI
JARDIN DU ROI
ORANGERIE

PORTE DES MATELOTS
ROUTE DE ST.CYR
CATHÉDRALE ST-LOUIS

N10
Pièce d'Eau des Suisses

© MICHAEL GRAHAM PUBLICATIONS

I am always glad to escape into the gardens. Possibly because waiting, often in a very long queue on the grassless, uneven front courtyard, seems to make all the marvellous opulence more of a duty rather than a pleasure. Love or hate the formality, there is a lot to see in one day. Originally Louis XIII used the mansion as a hunting lodge until his son Louis XIV, the 'Sun King', decided in 1664 to build a palace around it. In 1681 when his court had moved in, Louis XIV also began to run his government affairs from his new palace. He died at Versailles 34 years later. The palace became the most renowned in the world - a model for other royal residences. The magnificent apartments and galleries were designed under the direction of the painter Charles Le Brun. He used a lot of marble, gilded bronze and mirrors in the decoration. I suppose without doubt the most famous gallery is the Hall of Mirrors in the centre, at the rear of the palace, where there is a superb vista of the park. The domed ceiling of this gallery was painted by Le Brun himself. If you can, it is well worth seeing the Opéra room (1770), a masterpiece created by the architect, Jacques-Ange Gabriel. The Revolution closed the Palace until Napoleon reopened it, and then in 1837 it was made a museum.

Grand Trianon As you can see from the map, you can ride the little train to the château, take a good walk through the park, or travel by boat on the Grand Canal. The château was built by Louis XIV in 1688 as a refuge from the palace, and was designed in the Italian style. Later, Napoleon lived there after he had divorced Josephine.

Petit Trianon This small château was built in 1767 and was the place where the royal family gathered to entertain family and friends with music and games.

Hameau de la Reine The Queen's Hamlet consists of ten rustic cottages, grouped by a small lake. The largest cottage was the Queen's - Marie Antoinette's residence. The simple exterior was a contrast to the elegant interior. However, this was a real working Normandy style farm and the Queen and some of her followers reared poultry and made dairy produce - the profits from these she gave to the poor.

The Park The landscaping of the park was by the man responsible for the Tuileries Gardens, André Le Nôtre. From the palace, an unbroken vista leads the eye towards the Basin of Apollo and then to the Grand Canal. Turn right and walk towards the Basin of Neptune, which is the most spectacular fountain to be seen at Versailles. A 'Fête de Nuit', a spectacle with waterfalls, ballet, lighting and fireworks, is performed here on Saturdays from July through to September. On one side of the grand perspective in the grove you will discover the Salle de Bal, which has fountains and cascades: the central area was once covered with marble and used for dancing on summer evenings. The Colonnade nearby, with its marble columns, has basins spurting jets of water. Finally, before the Grand Canal is the Basin of Apollo, in which Apollo rises from the water in a chariot drawn by four horses. In mythology Apollo was supposed to commence his journey across the firmament at sunrise, bringing light to the world. The analogy is with Louis XIV, the 'Sun King'.

The easy way to reach Versailles is by RER (Métro) line number C5 to Versailles Rive Gauche.

Palace *9.00-17.30 (King's Room and Opéra guided tours only). Grand and Petit Trianon 10.00-12.30, 14.00-17.30. Closed Monday and some Bank Hols, Summer 18.30. Charge. Gardens open until dusk. Free*

ENTERTAINMENTS

For details of the events it is best to buy either Pariscope, the newspaper Figaro (for Figaroscope), or L'Officiel des Spectacles. The entertainment week begins on a Wednesday, and all these are available then. When booking at a theatre, if they say restricted view, they mean it! Three quarters of the stage could mean three quarters of the fire curtain.

Concert Halls

THÉÂTRE DES CHAMPS ÉLYSÉES   G4 29
15 Av. Montaigne, 75008.   ☎ (0)1.49.52.50.50
Completed in 1912, this is one of the first pre-stressed concrete buildings. It has sculpted reliefs by Antoine Bourdelle. The premiere performance of 'The Rite of Spring', by the Diaghilev company, was hooted off the stage here on the 29th May 1913.

CHÂTELET   B2 40
1 Place de Chatelet, 75001.   ☎ (0)1.40.28.28.40
Built in 1861 by Gabriel Davioud, this theatre is used for concerts, ballet and opera Often visiting American Broadway shows are staged here.

RADIO-FRANCE (Grand Auditorium) A3 36
116 Av. du Pres. Kennedy, 75016. ☎ (0)1.56.40.15.16
This has been the centre for French TV and radio since 1963. The hall has superb acoustics and is the home ground of a fine philharmonic orchestra.

SALLE PLEYEL   G6 21
252 Rue du Faubourg-St.Honoré. ☎ (0)8.25.00.08.21
75008. For many years this was the main concert hall in Paris, not only for classical music but for jazz as well. I expect many of us have recordings of music that took place here. Today the Orchestre de Paris have the Salle Pleyel as their home base.

Opera and Ballet

BASTILLE, OPÉRA DE PARIS   H4 41
2 Place de la Bastille, 75012.   ☎ (0)8.36.69.78.68
Designed by Carlos Ott, this huge 2700 seat monumental auditorium was opened on Bastille Day in 1989. The stage has been designed for easy scene changes, allowing three or four operas or ballets to be performed a week. The view from most seats is good and sound quality seems reasonable.

GARNIER. OPÉRA DE PARIS   F2 31
8 Rue Scribe, 75009.   ☎ (0)8.36.69.78.68
This magnificent building was designed by Charles Garnier. When it opened in 1875 it was the largest theatre in the world. Today, it still is impressive. The stage is enormous, both in width and depth, allowing for some spectacular scenic effects. The dome was painted in 1964 by the Russian Marc Chagall. It is light and balletic in style and a refreshing change from classical ceiling painting. Underneath the building is a water pocket, through which piles had to be driven when the foundations were being dug. This cavernous grotto in the basement is the source of the 'Phantom' legend. The policy of the Opéra de Paris is to stage operas at the Bastille theatre and use the Garnier for ballet. The price of tickets is very reasonable compared to some countries where opera and ballet are for the elite. Tours of the Opéra, performance permitting, are on: *Monday to Saturday 11.00 - 16.30 Charge*

OPÉRA COMIQUE   H2 31
5 Rue Favart, 75002.   ☎ (0)1.42.44.45.46
Built on the site of a previous theatre destroyed by fire, the building dates from 1899. This is the theatre to see lighter operas and ballets, including works by Offenbach, Strauss, Gounod and Delibes.

Ticket Agencies

Advance tickets can be booked at the Tourist Office (F2 29), or the Virgin Megastore (H3 29); both are situated in the Champs-Élysées. FNAC shops also sell tickets, otherwise try your hotel clerk. You can always go to the theatre, using a listing magazine to find the address and the index of this Mapguide.

TICKET KIOSQUE-THÉÂTRE   D3 30
15 Place Madeleine, 75008.   By the side of the Madeleine you will find the kiosk that sells same day tickets often at reduced prices. Another kiosk is located in the RER station Châtelet les Halles.
Tues to Fris 12.30-20.00, Saturday matinees 12.30.
Evenings 14.00-20.00, Suns 12.30-16.00 Closed Mons

Theatres

CASINO DE PARIS   F5 23
16 Rue de Clichy, 75009.   ☎ (0)1.49.95.99.99
A variety theatre where circuses, ballets, shows and artists from all over the world have performed.

CHAILLOT. THÉÂTRE NATIONAL DE D5 28
1 Place du Trocadéro, 75016. ☎ (0)1.53.65.30.00
Below the Palais de Chaillot is the Salle Jean Vilar. This seats 1200 people, and produces a wide variety of plays and shows. From the vestibule there is a superb view, over fountains, to the Eiffel Tower.

MOGADOR   F1 31
25 Rue de Mogador, 75009.   ☎ (0)1.53.32.32.00
A very large theatre that compares with the London Palladium. Often touring theatrical companies and musicals from America or Britain play here.

ODÉON. THÉÂTRE DE L'EUROPE   H5 39
1 Place Paul Claudel, 75006.   ☎ (0)1.44.41.36.36
Built by Chalgrin on the site of a previous theatre in 1818, it has an impressive portico with eight doric columns. The theatre seats 1040 people and has a reputation for its contemporary productions.

OLYMPIA   F3 31
28 Bd. des Capucines, 75009.   ☎ (0)1.47.42.25.49
The most famous music hall in Paris - Edith Piaf, Jean Sablon, Yves Montand all performed here.

Cinemas

Check after the film title to see if it says:
VF - this means the soundtrack is in French or
VO - the original soundtrack
So, if the stars are American and it says VO the soundtrack is in English. If they are Russian, the soundtrack is in Russian.
Here are a few of my favourite cinemas.

GAUMONT KINOPANORAMA   F4 37
60 Av. de la Motte-Picquet, 75015. A huge screen and sensational Dolby sound. ☎ (0)1.40.30.30.31

MAX LINDER PANORAMA   B2 32
24 Bd. Poissonnière, 75009.   ☎ (0)8.36.68.50.52
A very large screen and THX sound.

LA PAGODE   C4 38
57 rue de Babylone, 75007.   ☎ (0)1.45.55.48.48
Built in 1896 for a director of Bon Marché, since 1931 a cinema, now classified a historic monument.

LE GRAND REX   C3 32
1 Bd. Poissonnière, 75002.   ☎ (0)8.36.68.05.96
The original ceiling of stars and clouds, and a very large screen with comfortable seating for 2800 people, make this one of the best cinemas in Paris.

INDEX TO STREETS

ABBREVIATIONS *The letters following a name indicate the Square and Page Number*

Al.	-	Allée	Card.	-	Cardinal	Gén.	-	Général	Pte.	-	Porte
Arc.	-	Arcade	Col.	-	Colonel	Imp.	-	Impasse	R.	-	Rue
Av.	-	Avenue	Cdt.	-	Commandant	Mal.	-	Maréchal	St.	-	Saint
Bd.	-	Boulevard	Dr.	-	Docteur	Pas.	-	Passage	Ste.	-	Sainte
Cap.	-	Capitaine	Gal.	-	Galerie	Pl.	-	Place	Sq.	-	Square

HOUSE NUMBERING IN CENTRAL PARIS

Right Bank
↑ FROM THE SEINE NORTHWARDS

Left Bank
FROM THE SEINE SOUTHWARDS ↓

← FROM EAST TO WEST

Viewing the 3 directions, the even numbers are on the Right and the Odd numbers are on the Left

Bellini R. B6 28
Bellot R. H2 25
Belloy R. de D3 28
Belmondo R. Paul D4 48
Belvédère Av. du H3 27
Belzunce R. de D5 24
Ben-Aïad Pas. B4 32
Bénard R. D6 44
Benoist R. Marie F6 43
Benouville R. A3 28
Béranger R. G4 33
Béranger R. (P.St.G.) H2 27
Bérard Cour G3 41
Berbier du Mets R. C4 46
Bercy Bd. de C2 48
Bercy Quai de C4 48
Bercy R. de B2 48
Bergame Imp. de H3 43
Berger R. B6 32
Berger R. Georges A4 22
Bergère Cité et R. B2 32
Bergers R. des B6 36
Bergson Pl. Henri D6 22
Bérite R. de E5 39
Berlioz R. B1 28
Bernanos Av. Georges H2 45
Bernard Pl. Tristan D5 20
Bernard R. Claude C3 46
Bernard de Claivaux R. D6 32
Bern. de Ventadour R. C4 44
Bernardins R. des C4 40
Berne R. de D4 22
Bernouilli R. D4 22
Bernstein Pl. Leonard C3 48
Berri R. de H1 29
Berry Pl. Georges F1 31
Berryer Cité D3 30
Berryer R. G1 29
Bert R. Paul D4 42
Bertandeau Sq. Gaston D5 20
Berthaud Imp. D6 32
Berthe R. H3 23
Berthelot Pl. Marcelin B5 40
Berthier Bd. F2 21
Berthier Villa E3 21
Berthollet R. B3 46
Berthoud R. Ferdinand E4 33
Bertillon R. Alphonse A4 44
Berton R. B3 36
Bertrand Cité C4 34
Bertrand R. Guillaume C5 34
Bervic R. C3 24
Beslay Pas. B4 34
Béthune Quai de E4 41
Beudant R. C4 22
Bichat R. G2 33
Bidassoa R. de la F4 35
Bidault Ruelle C6 42
Bienfaisance R. de la C6 22
Bièvre R. de C4 40
Bineau Bd. B2 20
Binder R. de D3 26
Bingen R. Jacques A3 22
Biot R. E2 23
Birague R. de G3 41
Biscornet R. H4 41
Bisson R. C2 34
Bitche Pl. de C1 26
Bixio R. A3 38
Bizerte R. de D3 22
Bizet R. Georges F4 29
Blache R. Robert G6 25
Blainville R. C1 46
Blaise-Desgoffe R. E6 39
Blanc R. Lours G4 25
Blanc R. Louis (L.P.) E1 20
Blanche Imp. Marie G3 23
Blanche Pl. G3 23
Blanche R. F4 23
Blanche Villa A4 20
Blancs Manteaux R. des E1 41
Blanqui Bd. Auguste C6 46
Blanqui Villa Auguste C6 46
Blériot Quai Louis A4 36
Bleue R. C6 24
Blomet R. A1 44
Blondel R. D3 32
Bluets R. des D5 34
Blum Pl. Léon C1 42
Bobillot R. D6 46
Boccador R. de G4 29
Bochart de Saron R. A4 24
Boers Villa des E4 27
Boétie R. la B1 30
Bœuf Imp. du D1 40
Bœufs Imp. des C5 40
Boieldieu Pl. H2 31
Bois R. des H5 27
Bois de Boulogne R. du C1 28
Bois le Vent R. A2 36
Boisseau R. Guérin D4 32
Boissière R. D4 28
Boissière Villa D4 28
Boissieu R. C3 24
Boissonade R. G3 45

Boissy d'Anglas R. D3 30
Bolivar Av. Simon B6 26
Bolivar Sq. D6 26
Bologne R. Jean A2 36
Bonaparte R. G2 39
Bonheur R. Rosa A6 38
Bonne R. de la B2 24
Bonne Graine Pas. de la B4 42
Bonne Nouvelle Bd. de C3 32
Bonne Nouvelle Imp. de C2 32
Bonnet R. Louis B2 34
Bon Secours Imp. D3 42
Bons Enfants R. des H5 31
Bonsergent Pl. Jacques F2 33
Bonvin R. François H6 37
Borda R. E4 33
Bordais R. Jules F2 21
Borel R. Paul A3 22
Borey R. Elisa E4 35
Borghèse R. Pauline A2 20
Borrégo R. du H1 35
Borrégo Villa du H1 35
Bosquet Av. H2 37
Bosquet R. H2 37
Bosquet Villa G6 29
Bossuet R. D5 24
Bossut R. Charles D1 48
Botha R. E2 35
Bottin R. Sébastien F2 39
Botzaris R. D5 26
Bouchardon R. E2 33
Boucher R. de la B1 40
Bouchut R. A5 38
Boudreau R. F2 31
Bougainville R. A2 38
Boulainvilliers R. de A4 36
Boulanger Pl. Lili F4 23
Boulanger R. René F3 33
Boulangers R. des D6 40
Boulard R. F5 45
Boule Blanche Pas. de la A4 42
Boule Rouge Imp. de la B1 32
Boule Rouge R. de la B1 32
Boulets R. des F5 43
Boulle R. A4 42
Boulnois Pl. E5 21
Bouloi R. du A5 32
Bouquet de Longchamp D4 28
Rue du
Bourbon Quai de E3 41
Bourbon le Château R.de H3 39
Bourdaloue R. H6 23
Bourdan R. Pierre F6 43
Bourdelle R. Antoine C1 44
Bourdet R. Maurice A4 36
Bourdin Imp. H3 29
Bourdon Bd. E2 41
Bourdonnais Av. de la G2 37
Bourdonnais Imp. des B6 42
Bourdonnais R. des B1 40
Bouret R. B4 26
Bourg l'Abbé Pas. du C5 32
Bourg l'Abbé R. du D5 32
Bourgogne R. de C1 38
Bourg Tibourg R. du E2 41
Boursault R. et Imp. D3 22
Bourse Pl. de la A3 32
Bourse R. de la A3 32
Boussard Imp. Cordon G4 35
Boutarel R. D3 40
Boutebrie R. B4 40
Bouton R. Jean B6 42
Boutron Imp. F6 25
Bouvard Av. Joseph F2 37
Bouvart Imp. B5 40
Bouvier Rue E4 43
Bouvines R. de G4 43
Bouvines R. de G4 43
Boyer R. F3 35
Boyer-Barret R. C5 44
Boylesve Av. René B2 36
Brady Pas. E2 33
Brancusi Pl. D3 44
Branly Quai E1 37
Brantôme R. D6 32
Braque R. de F6 33
Braudel R.Fernand A4 48
Brazzaville Pl. de C4 36
Bréa R. F1 45
Bréguet R. B1 42
Bremontier R. G3 21
Brésil Pl. du G3 21
Bretagne R. de F5 33
Breteuil Av. de B4 38
Breteuil Pl. de B5 38
Breton R. Jules E3 47
Bretons Cour des A2 34
Brettonneau R. H4 35
Bretonvilliers R. de E4 41
Brey R. E6 21
Brézin R. E6 45
Briand R. Aristide C6 30

Briand R. Aristide (L.P.) B1 20
Briare Imp. B6 24
Bridaine R. D2 22
Brie Pas. de la A4 26
Brignole R. E4 29
Briquet Pas. B3 24
Briquet R. B3 24
Brisemiche R. D1 40
Brissac R. de G5 41
Brisson Pl. Pierre F4 29
Brizeux Sq. G3 35
Broca R. C3 46
Brochant R. C1 22
Brongniart R. A3 32
Brosse R. de D2 40
Brossolette R. Pierre C2 46
Brouillards Al. des H1 23
Broussais R. H6 45
Brown-Séguard R. B2 44
Bruant R. G4 47
Bruant R. Aristide G3 23
Brulon Pas. C4 42
Bruneau R. Alfred A2 36
Brunel R. D6 20
Brunetière Av. G1 21
Brunot Pl. Ferdinand E5 45
Brunoy Pas. B6 42
Bruxelles R. de F3 23
Brayère R. la G5 23
Bruyère Sq. la G5 23
Bucarest R. de E4 23
Bûcherie R. de la C3 40
Buci Carrefour de H3 39
Buci R. de H3 39
Budapest Pl. de E6 23
Budapest R. de E6 23
Budé R. E4 41
Budin R. Pierre D1 24
Buenos Ayres R. de D2 36
Buffault R. A6 24
Buffon R. F1 47
Bugeaud Av. B3 28
Buisson St. Louis R. du A2 34
Buisson St. Louis Pas. du A2 34
Bullet R. Pierre E2 33
Bullourde Pas. B3 42
Bureau Imp. et Pas. du F3 43
Burnouf R. A6 26
Burq R. H2 23
Buzelin R. G1 25
Buzenval R. de H4 43

C

Cabamel R. Alexandre G5 37
Cabanis R. H6 45
Cachot Sq. Albin B5 46
Cadet R. B6 24
Cadran Imp. du B3 24
Caffarelli R. F5 33
Cahors R. F2 27
Cail R. F4 25
Caillard Imp. B3 42
Caillié R. G3 25
Caire Av. César C6 22
Caire Pas. du C3 32
Caire Pl. du C3 32
Caire R. du D4 32
Calars R. de F4 23
Callot R. Jacques H2 39
Calvaire R. du A2 24
Calvaire R. du A2 24
Calvin R. Jean C2 46
Cambacérès R. C2 30
Cambo R. G6 27
Cambodge R. du G4 35
Cambon R. E3 31
Cambronne Pl. A5 38
Cambronne R. G6 37
Camoens Av. de C1 36
Campagne Première R. G3 45
Campo-Formio R. de F4 47
Camus Rue Albert H5 25
Canada R. du A5 30
Canada R. du F1 25
Candie R. du C4 42
Candole R. de C2 46
Canettes R. des G4 39
Cange R. du B5 44
Canivet R. du G4 39
Cantal Cour du A3 42
Capitaine Madon R. du E1 23
Cap. Ménard R. du B6 36
Cap. Scott R. du E3 37
Caplat R. D3 24
Caporal Peugeot R. du D2 20
Capron R. F2 23
Capucines Bd. des G2 31
Capucines R. des F3 31
Carco R. Francis E1 25
Card. Amette Pl. du E4 37
Card. Dubois R. du B2 24
Card. Guibert R. du A2 24

Card. Lemoine Cité du C5 40
Card. Lemoine R. du D5 40
Card. Mercier R. F4 23
Cardinale R. G3 39
Cardinet Pas. B2 22
Cardinet R. H3 21
Carducci R. E6 27
Carmes R. des C5 40
Carnot Av. E6 21
Carnot R. (P.St.G.) H2 27
Carnot Sq. G5 41
Carnot R. (Lev.Per.) D1 20
Carnot Villa Sadi G5 27
Caroline R. F3 41
Caron R. F3 41
Carpeaux R. F1 23
Carrel Pl. Armand C4 26
Carrel R. Alexis E3 37
Carrel R. Armand B4 26
Carrier-Belleuse R. G6 37
Carrière R. Eugène G1 23
Carrière-Mainguet Imp. E2 43
Carrières R. des B1 36
Carrières d'Amérique F3 37
Rue des
Carries R. Jean F3 37
Carrousel Pl. du G6 31
Casals. Rue Pablo B6 48
Casanova R.Danielle F3 31
Cascades R. des F2 35
Cassette R F5 39
Casent Pl. René B5 32
Cassini R. H4 45
Castagnary R. A5 44
Casteggio Imp. de G3 43
Castel Villa E2 35
Castelar R. Emilio B5 42
Castellane R. des E2 31
Castex R. G3 41
Castiglione R. de F4 31
Catalogne Pl. de C3 44
Catinat R. A4 32
Cauchois R. G3 23
Caulaincourt R. G2 23
Caulaincourt Sq. G1 23
Caumartin R. de F2 31
Cavarnac R. Godefroy C2 42
Cavalerie R. de F4 37
Cavallotti R. F2 23
Cavé R. D2 24
Cavendish R. C3 26
Cazotte R. B3 24
Célestins Quai des F3 41
Cels Imp. E4 45
Cels R. E4 45
Cendriers R. des E4 35
Censier R. D2 46
Cépré R. G6 37
Cerdan Pl. Marcel D4 36
Cerisaie R. de la G4 41
Cerisoles R. de G3 29
Cernuschi R. H2 21
César R. Jules H5 41
Cesselin Imp. D4 42
Cézanne R. Paul A1 30
Chabanais R. H4 31
Chablis R. de D4 48
Chabrier Sq. Emmanuel D3 22
Chabrol Cité de D6 24
Chabrol R. de D6 24
Chahu R. Claude B1 36
Chadlot R. de F4 29
Chaillot Sq. de F3 29
Chaise R. de la E3 39
Chalet R. du A1 34
Chagrin R. D1 28
Chalgny R. D5 42
Chalon Cour de B6 42
Chalon R. de B1 48
Chambertin R. de C2 48
Chambiges R. G4 29
Champagny R. de C2 38
Champaubert Av. de F4 37
Champerret C2 20
Av. de la Pte. de
Champerret D2 20
Pl. de la Pte. de
Champ de l'Alouette R.du B5 46
Champ de Mars R. du H2 37
Champfleury R. F3 37
Champollion R. A5 40
Champs-Elysées
Avenue des G2 29
Rond Point des A3 30
Champs Gal. des G2 29
Chanaleilles R. de D4 38
Chanc. Adenauer Pl. du A2 28
Chanoinesse R. C3 40
Chantier Pas. du A4 42
Chantiers R. des D5 40
Chantilly R. de C5 24
Chantres R. D3 40
Chanvin Pas. H5 47
Chanzy R. D3 42
Chapelle Av. de la C4 20
Chapelle Bd. de la F3 25

Name	Ref.
Rochambeau Pl.	E4 29
Rochambeau R.	B6 24
Rochebrune Pas.	C6 34
Rochebrune R.	C6 34
Rochechouart Bd. de	B3 24
Rochechouart R. de	B5 24
Rochefort R. Henri	A4 22
Rochefoucauld R.de la	G5 23
Rochefoucauld Sq.dela	D3 38
Rocher R. du	D6 22
Rocroy R. de	C5 24
Rodenbach Al.	H5 45
Rodier R.	B5 24
Roger R.	E4 45
Roger R. Edmond	D6 36
Rohan Cour de	A3 40
Rohan R. de	G5 31
Roi de Sicile R. du	E2 41
Roi Doré R. du	G1 41
Roi François Cour du	D4 32
Roll R. Alfred	G2 21
Rolleboise Imp.	H3 43
Rollin R.	C1 46
Rolinat Villa Maurice	F4 27
Romains R. Jules	B1 34
Romainville R. de	H6 27
Rome Cour de	E5 33
Rome R. de	D6 22
Rondeaux R. des	G5 35
Rondeaux Pas. des	G5 35
Rondelet R.	D6 42
Rondonneaux R. des	H5 35
Ronsard R.	B3 24
Ronsin Imp.	B1 44
Roosevelt Av. Franklin D.	A3 30
Roquépine R.	C1 30
Roquette Cité de la	A3 42
Roquette R. de la	B2 42
Roret R. Nicolas	D4 46
Rosenwald R.	A4 44
Rosière R. de la	D6 36
Rosiers R. des	F2 41
Rossini R.	H2 31
Rostand Pl.Edmond	A5 40
Rostand Pl. Jean	B2 34
Rothschild Imp.	E2 23
Rotrou R.	H4 39
Rouault Al. Georges	D3 34
Roubaix Pl. de	D4 24
Roubo R.	E4 43
Rouché Pl. Jacques	G2 31
Rouelle R.	D5 36
Rouen R. de	B2 26
Rougemont Cité	B2 32
Rougemont R.	B2 32
Rouget de l'Isle R.	E4 31
Roule Av. du	A4 20
Roule R. du	B6 32
Roule Sq. du (8e)	F6 21
Roule Sq. du (Neuilly)	A3 20
Rouquier R. Louis	C1 20
Rousseau R. Jean-Jacques	A5 32
Roussel R. Théophile	B4 42
Rousselet R.	C5 38
Rouvier R. Maurice	A6 44
Rouvray R. de	B2 20
Roux Pas.	F4 21
Roy R.	C1 30
Royale Rue & Galerie	D3 30
Royer-Collard Imp.	A6 40
Royer-Collard R.	A6 40
Rozier R. Arthur	F5 27
Rubens R.	E5 47
Rude R.	D1 28
Rueff Pl. Jacques	F2 37
Ruelle Pas.	E2 25
Ruelle Sourdis	F6 33
Ruffin Imp.	H3 29
Ruhmkorff R.	C4 20
Rutebeuf Pl.	B1 48
Ruysdaël Av.	A5 22

S

Name	Ref.
Sablière R. de la	D5 44
Sablons R. des	B4 28
Sablonville R. de	A4 20
Sabot R. du	F3 39
Saché R. Georges	D5 44
Sacre Cœur Cité du	A2 24
Saïd Villa	A1 28
Saigon R. de	D1 28
Saillard R.	E5 45
St. Amand R.	A4 44
St. Ambroise Pas.	B5 34
St. Ambroise R.	B6 34
St. André des Arts Place et Rue	A3 40
St. Antoine Pas.	B3 42
St. Antoine R.	G3 41
St. Augustin Pl.	D1 30
St. Augustin R.	H3 31
St. Benoit R.	G2 39
St. Bernard Pas.	C4 42
St. Bernard Quai	F6 41
St. Bernard R.	C3 42
St. Bon R.	C1 40
St. Bruno R.	E2 24
St. Charles Imp.	B6 36
St. Charles Pl.	C5 36
St. Charles R.	D4 36
St. Chaumont Cité	B1 34
St. Christophe R.	A6 36
St. Claude Imp.	G6 33
St. Claude R.	G6 33
St. Denis Bd.	D3 32
St. Denis Imp.	C4 32
St. Denis Porte	D3 32
St. Denis R.	D4 32
St. Didier R.	C4 28
St. Dominique R.	B1 38
Ste. Anastase R.	G1 41
Ste. Anne Pas.	H3 31
Ste. Anne R.	G4 31
Ste. Anne Popincourt Pas.	H1 41
Ste. Apolline R.	D3 32
Ste. Avoie Pas.	F6 33
Ste. Beuve R.	F1 45
Ste. Cécile R.	B2 32
Ste. Croix de la Bretonnerie Rue et Square	D1 40
Ste. Élisabeth Pas.et R.	F4 33
Ste. Foy Pas et Rue	D3 32
Ste. Geneviève Pl.	C6 40
Ste. Éleuthère R.	A2 24
St. Éloi Cour	E5 43
Ste. Lucie R.	C6 36
Ste. Marthe Imp. et Rue	A1 34
Ste. Opportune Pl. et R.	C1 40
St. Esprit Cour du	B4 42
St. Étienne du Mont R.	C6 40
St. Eustache Imp.	B5 32
St. Fargeau R.	H2 35
St. Ferdinand Pl.	C5 20
St. Ferdinand R.	D5 20
St. Fiacre Imp.	C1 40
St. Fiacre R.	B3 32
St. Florentin R.	E4 31
St. Georges Pl.	H5 23
St. Georges R.	H6 23
St. Germain Bd.	E2 39
St. Germ. l'Auxerrois R.	B1 40
St. Gervais Pl.	D2 40
St. Gilles R.	G1 41
St. Gothard R. du	G6 45
St. Guillaume R.	F3 39
St. Hippolyte R.	B4 46
St. Honoré R.	F4 31
St. Honoré d'Eylau Av.	C4 28
St. Hubert R.	C5 34
St. Hyacinthe R.	F4 31
St. Irénée Sq.	B6 34
St. Jacques Bd.	H5 45
St. Jacques Cour	A3 42
St. Jacques Pl.	G5 45
St. Jacques R.	B4 40
St. Jacques Villa	G5 45
St. Jean R.	E1 23
St. Jean Baptiste de La Salle Rue	D5 38
St. Jérôme R.	D2 24
St. Joseph Cour	A3 42
St. Joseph R.	B3 32
St. Josse R.	C6 32
St. Julien le Pauvre R.	C4 40
St. Laurent R.	D5 24
St. Lazare R.	F6 23
St. Léonie Imp.	D5 44
St. Louis Cour	A3 42
St. Louis en l'Isle R.	E4 41
St. Luc R.	D2 24
St. Mandé Av. de	H6 43
St. Mandé Villa	H6 43
St. Marc R.	A3 32
St. Marceaux R. de	G1 21
St. Marcel Bd.	E3 47
St. Martin Bd.	F3 33
St. Martin Cité	E2 33
St. Martin Porte	E3 33
St. Martin R.	D5 32
St. Mathieu R.	E2 25
St. Maur Pas.	B5 34
St. Maur R.	B3 34
St. Médard R.	C1 46
St. Merri R.	D1 40
St. Michel Bd.	A5 40
St. Michel Quai	B3 40
St. Michel Pas.	E1 23
St. Michel Pl.	B3 40
St. Michel Villa	E1 23
St. Nicolas Cour	E4 43
St. Nicolas R.	A4 42
Saintonge R. de	G5 33
St. Ouen Av. de	E1 23
St. Paul Pas. et R.	F3 41
St. Philippe R.	C3 32
St. Philippe du Roule Passage et Rue	A2 30
St. Pierre Cour	E2 23
St. Pierre Imp.	H3 43
St. Pierre R.	B3 24
St. Pierre Amelot Pas.	H5 33
St. Placide R.	E5 39
St. Quentin R. de	E5 25
St. Roch Pas. et R.	G4 31
St. Romain R. et Sq.	D5 38
St. Rustique R.	A2 24
St. Sabin Pas.	A2 42
St. Sabin R.	H1 41
Saint Saëns R.	D3 36
St. Sauveur R.	C4 32
St. Sébastien Imp.	A6 34
St. Sébastien Pas. et R.	H6 33
St. Senoch R. de	E4 21
St. Séverin R.	B4 40
St. Simon R. de	E2 39
St. Simoniens Pas.des	G2 35
Saints Pères R. des	C3 32
St. Spire R.	C3 32
St. Sulpice Pl. et R.	G4 39
St. Thomas d'Aquin R.	E2 39
St. Victor R.	D5 40
St. Vincent Imp.	D5 26
St. Vincent R.	A2 24
St. Vincent de Paul R.	D4 24
Salarnier Pas.	A2 42
Salneuve R.	B3 22
Salomon de Caus R.	D4 32
Salonique Av. de	B4 20
Samain R. Albert	E2 27
Sambre et Meuse R. de	A1 34
Sampaix R. Lucien	F2 33
Sandrié Imp.	F2 31
Sansbœuf R. Joseph	D1 30
Santé Imp. de la	A4 46
Santé R. de la	A5 46
Santeuil R.	D3 46
Santiago du Chile Pl.	A1 38
Sarcey R. Francisque	B1 36
Sarrazin R. Pierre	A4 40
Satie R. Erik	D3 26
Satragne Sq. Alban	D1 32
Sauffroy R.	D1 22
Saules R. des	A1 24
Saulnier R.	B1 32
Saunière R. Paul	B1 36
Saussaies R. et R. des	C2 30
Saussier-Leroy R.	E5 21
Saussure R. de	B2 22
Sauton R. Frédéric	C4 40
Sauval R.	A6 32
Savart R. Laurence	E2 35
Savies R. de	A3 40
Savoie R. de	C5 40
Savorgnan de Brazza R.	G3 37
Saxe Av. de	A5 38
Saxe Villa de	A4 24
Say R.	H1 41
Scarron R.	G1 41
Scheffer R. de	B6 28
Scheffer Villa	A5 28
Schœlcher R.	F4 45
Schomberg R. de	F5 41
Schumann Av. Robert	A6 30
Schutzenberger R.	C4 36
Scipion R.	D3 46
Scotto R. Vincent	B2 26
Scribe R.	F2 31
Sébastopol Bd. de	D4 32
Secrétan Av.	A4 26
Sécurité Pas.	E5 37
Sedaine Cour et Rue	B2 42
Sédillot R.	G1 37
Sédillot Sq.	G1 37
Séguier R.	A3 40
Ségur Av. de	A4 38
Ségur Villa de	A4 38
Seine Quai de la	B2 26
Seine R. de	H3 39
Séjourné R. Paul	G2 45
Selves Av. de	B3 30
Semanaz R.	H3 27
Semard R. Jean Baptiste	
Semard R. Pierre	C5 24
Sénégal R. de	C2 34
Senlis R. de	F2 21
Sente des Dorées	F2 27
Sentier R. du	C4 44
Séoul Pl. de	A1 38
Sept Arpents R. des	H1 27
Serpente R.	A4 40
Sérurier Bd.	G2 27
Servan R. et Sq.	C6 34
Servandoni R.	G4 39
Severo R.	E5 45
Seveste R.	B3 24
Sévigné R. de	F2 41
Sèvres R. de	D5 38
Sèze R. de	E3 31
Sfax R. de	C2 28
Shaw R. G. Bernard	E4 37
Sibour R.	E1 33
Signac Pl. Paul	H3 35
Signac R.	B3 24
Silvestre de Sacy Av.	F1 37
Simart R.	C1 24
Simonnot R.	H3 27
Simon Villa Adrienne	E4 45
Simon le Franc R.	D1 40
Singer R.	A2 36
Singes Pas. des	E1 41
Sisley R.	G1 21
Sivel R.	E5 45
Sœur Catherine Marie Rue	B6 46
Sœur Rosalie Av. de la	D5 46
Sofia R. de	C3 24
Soissons R de	A3 26
Soleil R. du	G1 35
Soleillet R.	F4 35
Solférino R de	D1 38
Solidarité R. de la	F3 27
Solitaires R. des	E6 27
Somme Bd. de la	D2 20
Sommerard R. du	B4 40
Sontay R. de	C3 28
Sorbier R.	F4 35
Sorbonne Pl. de la	A5 40
Sorbonne R. de la	B5 40
Souchet Villa	H4 35
Souchier Villa	A5 28
Soudan R. de	E4 37
Soufflot R.	B6 40
Souhaits Imp. des	H3 43
Soupirs Pas. des	G3 35
Sourdière R. de la	G4 31
Souvenir Français Esplanade du	B3 37
Souzy Cité	E4 43
Spinelli R. Crocé	C4 44
Spinoza R.	D5 34
Spontini R.	A3 28
Spontini Villa	A3 28
Spuller R. Eugène	F5 33
Staël R. de	A1 44
Stalingrad Place de la Bataille de	H3 25
Stalingrad R. de	H2 27
Stanislas R.	F1 45
Steinkerque R. de	B3 24
Steinlen R.	A2 24
Stemler Cité	B1 34
Stendhal Pas.	H6 35
Rue et Villa	H6 35
Stephenson R.	E2 25
Stern R. Daniel	E4 37
Stevens Pas. Alfred	H4 23
Stevens R. Alfred	H4 23
Stockholm R. de	D6 22
Strasbourg Bd. de	E1 33
Strauss Pl. Johann	F3 33
Stravinsky Pl. Igor	D1 40
Stuart R. Marie	C5 32
Sud Pas. du	C3 26
Sue R. Eugène	B1 24
Suez Imp.	H1 43
Suez R. de	D2 24
Suffren Av. de	G5 37
Suger R.	A3 40
Suisses R. des	B6 44
Sully R. de	G4 41
Sully-Prudhomme Av.	A6 30
Surcouf R.	A6 30
Surène R. de	D2 30
Surmelin R. du	H3 35
Sylvia R. Gaby	H1 41

T

Name	Ref.
Tacherie R. de la	C2 40
Taclet R.	G2 35
Tahan R. Camille	F2 23
Taillade Av.	F1 35
Taillandiers Pas. des	B3 42
Taillandiers R. des	B3 42
Tailbourg Av. de	G5 43
Taitbout R.	G1 31
Talleyrand R. de	B1 38
Talma R.	A2 36
Talon R. Omer	D6 34
Tandou R.	F2 27
Tanger R. de	H2 25
Tanneries R. des	B5 46
Tapisseries R. des	H1 21
Tarbé R.	B2 22
Tardieu Pl. André	B4 38
Tarn Sq. du	F1 21
Taylor R.	E3 33
Téhéran R. de	B6 22
Teilhard de Chardin R.	C2 46
Télégraphe Pas. du	G1 35
Télégraphe R. du	H2 35
Tell R. Guillaume	E3 21
Temple Bd. du	G5 33

Temple R. du	F5 33	Trébois R.	D1 20	Varsovie Pl. de	D6 28	Ville l'Evêque R. de la	D2 30
Tenailles Pas.	E5 45	Trefouel	B2 44	Vauban Pl.	B2 38	Villemain Av.	C5 44
Ternaux R.	A5 34	Pl. Jacques et Thérèse		Vaucanson R.	E4 33	Ville Neuve R. de la	C3 32
Ternes Av. des	D5 20	Treilhard R.	B6 22	Vaucluse Sq. de	F1 21	Villermé R. René	D6 34
Ternes Pl. des	F5 21	Trélat R. Ulysse	B6 48	Vaucouleurs R. de	B3 34	Villersexel R. de	E1 39
Ternes R. des	D4 20	Trémoille R. de la	G4 29	Vaudoyer R. Léon	A5 38	Villesexel R. de la	E5 27
Ternes Villa des	C4 20	Trésor R. du	E2 41	Vaugirard Bd. de	C2 44	Villette Bd. de la	A6 26
Terrage R. du	F6 25	Trévise Cité et R. de	B1 32	Vaugirard R. de	G5 39	Villette R. de la	E5 27
Terrasse R. de la	B4 22	Trinité Pas. de la	D4 32	Vauquelin R.	C2 46	Villey R. Pierre	H1 37
Terrasse Villa de la	B4 22	Trinité R. de la	F5 23	Vauvilliers R.	B6 32	Villiers Av. de	H3 21
Terre Neuve R. de	G3 43	Trocadéro Sq. du	B5 28	Vavin Av.	G1 45	Villiers Av.de la Pte. de	C3 20
Tertre Imp. et Pl. du	A2 24	Trocadéro et du 11 Novembre		Vavin R.	F1 45	Villiers Bd. de	B2 20
Tesson R.	A2 34	Place du	C5 28	Velasquez Av.	B5 22	Villiers R. de	B2 20
Texel R. de	D4 44	Trois Bornes		Vellefaux Av. Claude	H1 33	Villiers de l'IsleAdam R.	G3 35
Thann R. de	A4 22	Cité et Rue des	A4 34	Vendôme Cour et Pl.	F4 31	Impasse	H3 35
Théâtre R. du	D5 36	Trois Couronnes R. des	B3 34	Vendôme Pas.	G4 33	Villin R.	D3 34
Thébaud Sq. Jean	G6 37	Trois Frères Cour de	B4 42	Vénézuela Pl. du	C2 28	Villiot R.	B2 48
Thénard R.	B4 40	Trois Frères R. des	A3 24	Venise R. de	C6 32	Vimoutiers R. de	A5 48
Théodore de Banville R.	F4 21	Trois Portes R. des	C4 40	Ventadour R. de	G4 31	Vinaigriers R. des	F1 33
Thérèse R.	G4 31	Trois Soeurs Imp. des	B1 40	Véran Imp.	G3 43	Vincennes Cours de	H5 43
Thermopyles R. des	G4 43	Trois Visages Imp. des	B1 40	Vercingétorix R.	C4 44	Vineuse R.	C6 28
Thibaud R.	E6 45	Tronchet R.	E2 31	Verdeau Pas.	A1 32	29 Juillet R. du	F5 31
Thiéré Pas.	A3 42	Trône Av. et Pas. du	G5 43	Verdun Av. de	F6 25	Vintimille R. de	F4 23
Thierry R. Augustin	F6 27	Tronson du Coudray R.	D2 30	Verdun Pl. de	A5 20	Violet Pl.	D6 36
Thiers Rue et Sq.	A4 28	Trousseau R.	C3 42	Verdun R. de	F6 25	Violet R.	E5 37
Thimerais Sq. du	F2 21	Troyon R.	E6 21	Vergniaud R.	B6 46	Viollet le Duc R.	A4 24
Thimonnier R.	B5 24	Truchet R. Abel	E3 23	Vergniaud R. (Lev. Per.)	B2 20	Visconti R.	G2 39
Thionville Pas. de	C2 26	Trudaine Av.	B4 24	Verhaeren Al.	H5 45	Visitation Pas. de la	D2 38
Thionville R. de	D1 26	Trudaine Sq.	A5 24	Verlaine Villa Paul	E4 27	Vital R.	A1 36
Tholozé R.	G2 23	Truffaut R.	D2 22	Verlomme R. Roger	G2 41	Vitruve R.	H2 43
Thomas R. Albert	F3 33	Truffaut R. François	D5 48	Vermandois Sq. du	G4 27	Vitu R. Auguste	A6 36
Thomas R. Ambroise	C1 32	Truillot Imp.	B6 34	Vermenouze Sq.	C2 46	Vivarais Sq. du	C3 20
Thomas R. Yéo	F6 47	Tuck Av. Edward	C4 30	Verne R. Jules	B3 34	Vivienne Gal.	H4 31
Thorel R.	C3 32	Tuileries Quai des	E5 31	Vernet R.	F2 29	Vivienne R.	H3 31
Thorigny Pl. et Rue de	F1 41	Tunis R. de	G5 43	Verneuil R. de	F2 39	Voisin R. Félix	E1 43
Thouin R.	C6 40	Tunnel R. du	D5 26	Vernier R.	D3 20	Vollon R. Antoine	B4 42
Thuillier R. Louis	B1 46	Turbigo R. de	E4 33	Verniquet R.	G2 21	Volney R.	F3 31
Thuliez R. Louise	F6 27	Turenne R. de	G1 41	Véro-Dodat Gal.	A5 32	Volontaires R. des	A2 44
Thuré Cité	E6 37	Turgot R.	B4 24	Véron Cité	F3 23	Volta R.	E4 33
Tillier R. Claude	B1 46	Turin R. de	E5 23	Véron R.	G3 23	Voltaire Bd.	C2 42
Tilsitt R. de	E1 29	Turot R. Henri	A6 26	Véronèse R.	D5 46	Voltaire Cité	F3 43
Timbaud R. Jean-Pierre	B4 34	Turquetil Pas.	F4 43	Verrerie R. de la	D2 40	Voltaire Quai	F1 39
Tiphaine R.	E5 37			Versailles Av. de	A4 36	Voltaire R. (Ile)	F3 43
Tiquetonne R.	C5 32	**U**		Vertbois R. du	E4 33	Voltaire R. (Lev. Per.)	B2 20
Tiron R.	E2 41	Ulm R. d'	B1 46	Verte Al.	H1 41	Vosges R. des	G2 41
Tison R. Jean	A6 32	Union Pas. de l'	H2 37	Vertus R. des	E5 33	Vouillé R. de	A5 44
Titien R.	E4 47	Union Sq. de l'	C4 28	Verzy Av. de	D3 46	Voulzie R. de la	F4 35
Titon R.	D4 42	Université R. de l'	H6 29	Vésale R.	D3 46	Vrillière R.La	A4 32
Tlemcen R. de	E4 35	Ursins R. des	D3 40	Vexin Sq. du	G4 27	Vulpian R.	B6 46
Tocqueville R. de	A2 22	Ursulines R. des	A1 46	Vézelay R. de	B5 22		
Tocqueville Sq. de	H2 21	Uruguay Pl. de l'	E3 29	Viala R.	D4 36	**W**	
Tolbiac R. de	B6 48	Utrillo R. Maurice	B2 24	Viallet Pas.	C2 42	Wagram Av. de	G4 21
Tombe-Issoire R. de la	G6 45	Uzès R. d'	B3 32	Vian R. Boris	D3 24	Wagram Pl. de	G2 21
Tombouctou R. de	E3 25			Viarmes R. de	A5 32	Wagram-St.Honor Villa	F6 21
Torcy R. de	F1 25	**V**		Vicaire R. Gabriel	F5 33	Waldeck-Rousseau R.	C5 20
Torricelli R.	D4 20	Vacquerie R. Auguste	E3 29	Vicq d'Azir R.	H6 25	Wallons R. des	F3 47
Toudic R. Yves	G5 33	Vacquerie R. La	D1 42	Victoire R. de la	H1 31	Washington R.	G1 29
Toudouze Pl. Gustave	H5 23	Valadon R.	H2 37	Victoires Pl. des	A4 32	Watteau R.	E4 47
Toullier R.	B5 40	Valadon Pl. Suzanne	A3 24	Victoria Av.	C2 40	Wauxhall Cité du	F3 33
Toulouse R. de	G3 27	Val de Grâce R. du	A2 46	Vieille du Temple R.	F1 41	Weber R.	B2 28
Tour R. de la	A6 28	Valence R. de	C3 46	Vienne R. de	D5 22	Weiss R. Charles	A5 44
Tour d'Auvergne	A5 24	Valenciennes Pl.de	D5 24	Vierge Pas. de la	H2 37	Weiss R. Louise	H6 47
Impasse et Rue de la		Valenciennes R. de	E5 25	Vierne R. Louis	D2 20	Westermann R.	F4 35
Tour des Dames	G5 23	Valentin R. Edmond	G1 37	Viete R.	H3 21		
R. de la		Valéry R. Paul	D3 28	Vieuville R. La	H3 23	**X**	
Tour de Vanves	D4 44	Valette R.	B5 40	Vieux Colombier R. du	F4 39	Xaintrailles R.	H6 47
Pas. de la		Valhubert Pl.	G1 47	Vigée-Lebrun R.	A3 44		
Tourlaque R.	G2 23	Vallès R. Jules	D3 42	Vignes R. des	A3 36	**Y**	
Tour-Maubourg	A2 38	Vallet Pas.	F5 47	Vignoles Imp. et R.des	H2 43	Yorktown Sq. de	C6 28
Bd. et Sq. de la		Valmy Imp de	E3 39	Vignon R.	E2 31	Yser Bd. de l'	C3 20
Tournefort R.	C1 46	Valmy Quai de	H4 25	Viguès Cour	A4 42	Yves du Manoir Av.	C4 20
Tournelle Quai de la	D4 40	Valois Av. de	B5 22	Viguès Cour Jacques	A3 42		
Tournelles R. des	G2 41	Valois Pl. et Rue de	H5 31	Village Suisse Le	F4 37	**Z**	
Tournemire R.Charles	C3 20	Valpeau R.	E3 39	Villaceau R. Yvon	C3 28	Zay R. Jean	D3 44
Tournon R. de	H4 39	Vandamme R.	D3 44	Villaret de Joyeuse R.	D6 20	Zeit Pas.	E2 33
Tournus R.	E5 37	Van Dyck Av.	H5 21	Villaret de Joyeuse Sq.	D6 20	Zelenski R. Boy	H6 25
Tourtille R. de	C2 34	Vaneau Cité	C3 38	Villars Av. de	B4 38	Ziem R. Félix	G1 23
Tourville Av. de	B3 38	Vaneau R.	D5 38	Ville R. Georges	D3 28	Zola R. Émile	D6 36
Toustain R.	H4 39	Van Gogh R.	A1 48	Villebois-Mareuil R.	E5 21	Zola Sq. Émile	C5 36
Tracy R. de	D3 32	Varenne Cité et R. de	D3 38	Villedo R.	H4 31		
Traktir R. de	D2 28	Varèse R. Edgar	E1 27	Villehardouin R.	G1 41		
Transvaal R. du	E2 35	Varlin R. Eugène	G5 25				
Traversière R.	A5 42						

Cover and Page 1 Illustrations
by Ronald Maddox PRI, FCSD.

PENGUIN BOOKS

First published 1994
Second Edition published 2002
3 4 5 6 7 8 9 10
Revised 2004

Published by the Penguin Group
Penguin Books Ltd, 80 Strand, London WC2R 0RL, England
Penguin Putnam Inc., 375 Hudson Street, New York, New York 10014, USA
Penguin Books Australia Ltd, 250 Camberwell Road, Camberwell, Victoria 3124, Australia
Penguin Books Canada Ltd, 10 Alcorn Avenue, Toronto, Ontario, Canada M4V 3B2
Penguin Books India (P) Ltd, 11 Community Centre, Panchsheel Park, New Delhi - 110 017, India
Penguin Books (NZ) Ltd, Cnr. Rosedale and Airborne Roads, Albany, Auckland, New Zealand
Penguin Books (South Africa) (Pty) Ltd, 24 Sturdee Avenue, Rosebank 2196, South Africa
Penguin Books Ltd, Registered Offices: 80 Strand, London WC2R 0RL, England

MICHAEL GRAHAM PUBLICATIONS